STECK-VAUGHN

LIFE Skills

FOR TODAY'S WORLD

BY VIVIAN BERNSTEIN

Community and Government

CONSULTANTS

Dee Marie Boydstun
Literacy Coordinator
Black Hawk College
Moline, Illinois

Marie S. Olsen
Learning Center Coordinator
for Rio Salado Community College
at Maricopa Skill Center
Phoenix, Arizona

John C. Ritter
Teacher, Education Programs
Oregon Women's Correctional Center
Salem, Oregon

STECK-VAUGHN®
COMPANY
A Subsidiary of National Education Corporation

ABOUT THE AUTHOR

Vivian Bernstein is the author of *America's Story, World History and You, World Geography and You, American Government*, and *Decisions for Health*. She received her Master of Arts degree from New York University. Bernstein is active with professional organizations in social studies, education, and reading. She gives presentations to school faculties and professional groups about content area reading. Bernstein was a teacher in the New York City Public School System for a number of years.

ACKNOWLEDGMENTS

Executive Editor: Diane Sharpe
Project Editor: Anne Souby
Designer: Pamela Heaney
Photo Editor: Margie Foster
Production: American Composition & Graphics, Inc.

CREDITS

Cover Photography: © Comstock

p. 5 © Tony Freeman/PhotoEdit; p. 6 Washington Area Convention & Visitors Bureau; p. 9L © Elizabeth Crews/Stock Boston; p. 9R © David Young-Wolff/PhotoEdit; p. 11 Cooke Photographics; p. 16 © Michael Newman/PhotoEdit; p. 17 © Anna Kaufman Moon/Stock Boston; p. 18 © Grant Leduc/Stock Boston; pp. 26, 29 © Bob Daemmrich/Stock Boston; p. 36 Park Street; p. 37 © Ellis Herwig/Stock Boston; p. 39 © Gale Zucker/ Stock Boston; p. 40 © Bob Daemmrich/Stock Boston; pp. 46, 47 Park Street; p. 50 © Charles Feil/Stock Boston; p. 51 © Stacy Pick/Stock Boston; p. 57 Park Street; p. 59 © Michael Newman/PhotoEdit; p. 61 (all) Park Street; p. 63 © Martin Rogers/Stock Boston; p. 68 Park Street; p. 71 © Erika Stone/Photo Researchers; p. 72 © Ellis Herwig/Stock Boston; p. 78 © Barbara Rios/Photo Researchers; p. 79 © Bob Krueger/Photo Researchers; p. 80 Park Street; p. 81 © Mark Richards/PhotoEdit.

We would like to express our appreciation to all local, state, and national governmental agencies that helped in the preparation of this book. In particular, we would like to thank the following for providing information and forms for the workshops:

    Florida Office of the Governor
    Vital Records Office, Arkansas Department of Health
    Marion County District Court, State of Oregon
    Equal Employment Opportunity Commission
    Police Department, County of Nassau, New York
    Social Security Administration
    California Secretary of State's Office

CONTENTS

Life Skills for Today's World is a series of five books. These books are *Money and Consumers*, *The World of Work*, *Your Own Home*, *Personal Health*, and *Community and Government*. They can help you learn skills to be successful in today's world and will show you how to use these skills in your daily life.

This book is *Community and Government*. Each chapter in this book has six pages of lesson text. This text is followed by a workshop and exercises. One workshop in this book is "Completing a Voter Registration Form." What kind of government forms have you filled out?

_____

_____

_____

In the "Thinking and Writing" exercise, you will be asked to write in your journal. Your journal can be a notebook or just a group of papers. Writing in a journal helps you gather your thoughts and put them on paper. One exercise in this book asks you to think about how government could save money. Thinking and writing about problems can help you find answers. Try it here. Think about questions or problems you may have about dealing with the government. On the lines below, tell how you think this book will help you.

_____

_____

_____

There are an index, a glossary, and an answer key in the back of this book. These features can help you use this book independently.

Have fun working through this book. Then enjoy your new skills!

AMERICAN GOVERNMENT

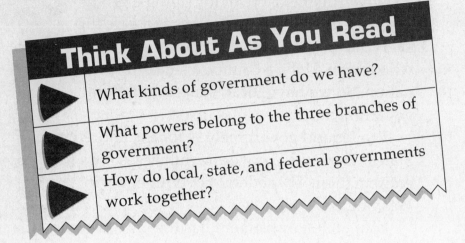

Think About As You Read

▶ What kinds of government do we have?

▶ What powers belong to the three branches of government?

▶ How do local, state, and federal governments work together?

On the first Tuesday in November, Donna Cole voted. She voted for her choice for a president and a governor. She voted for her choices for **legislators** and judges. To make smart choices, Donna needed to know how these different jobs fit into the American plan of government. She needed to know if she was voting for a legislator for her state or for the nation.

Legislators are lawmakers.

The American people choose their government leaders by voting.

5

In this chapter you will learn about how American government has been planned to run your country, state, and community.

Different Kinds of Government

Government is a plan for ruling a group of people. The rules try to protect and care for everyone in the group. The group may be the people who live in a city, a county, a state, or the whole nation. So we have **local**, state, and **federal** governments.

The federal government is for the entire United States. The federal government passes laws for the entire nation. The federal government is in Washington, D.C.

Your state government has the job of running the state. Each of the fifty states in the United States has its own government. Each state has its own state **constitution**.

Local governments take care of running your city and county. You may be part of other local governments, too.

Three Branches of Government

The plan for governing the nation is the United States Constitution. The Constitution has a plan for three **branches** of government. Each branch has its

Local governments are the governments for cities, towns, counties, villages, and other regions in a state.

The **federal government** is the government for the entire nation. It is in Washington, D.C. It shares power with state and local governments.

A **constitution** is a plan for government.

Branches are parts of a whole. There are three branches of government.

The United States Capitol in Washington, D.C., is where Congress meets.

own powers. This plan makes sure that no one person or branch can have too much power. This plan protects the rights and freedom of the American people.

The **legislative** branch writes the laws. This branch of the federal government is called **Congress**. Congress is made up of two houses. The two houses of Congress are the Senate and the House of Representatives.

Legislators in the Senate are called **senators**. Every state sends two senators to Congress. Legislators in the House of Representatives are called **representatives**. Each state has a different number of representatives in the House of Representatives. States with more people have more representatives than states with fewer people. People in every state vote for senators and representatives to make laws for the nation. Laws must be passed by both the Senate and the House of Representatives.

The second branch is called the **executive** branch. This branch carries out the laws. The President of the United States is the leader of the executive branch of the federal government.

Legislative means lawmaking. One of the three branches of government is the legislative branch.

Congress makes the laws for the United States. It is the legislative branch of the federal government.

Senators are lawmakers. They serve in the Senate.

A **representative** is a lawmaker who serves in the House of Representatives.

The **executive** branch is one of the three branches of government. The executive branch carries out the laws written by the legislative branch.

Three Branches of Federal Government

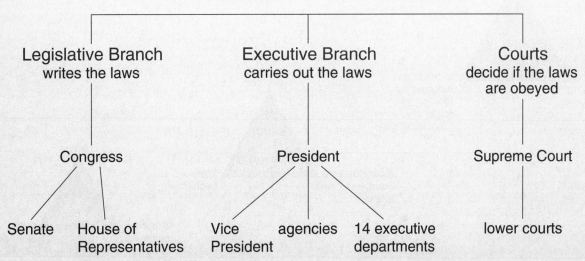

Legislative Branch
writes the laws

Executive Branch
carries out the laws

Courts
decide if the laws
are obeyed

Congress

President

Supreme Court

Senate   House of
Representatives

Vice   agencies   14 executive
President   departments

lower courts

Agencies are large groups of people in the government that work together to do certain kinds of work.

The executive branch has many **agencies** to help carry out the law. For example, Congress passes tax laws. The executive branch carries out those laws by collecting taxes. The job of collecting taxes is carried out by an executive agency. That agency is the Internal Revenue Service, or IRS.

The courts make up the third branch of government. The courts decide if people have obeyed the laws. This branch also makes sure that the laws agree with the Constitution.

The United States Supreme Court is the nation's most powerful court. Nine judges work on the Supreme Court. Before a case can be decided by the Supreme Court, it must first be judged in lower courts. State and federal laws must be changed if the Supreme Court decides they are wrong.

The plans for many state and local governments are similar to the plan for the federal government. State and local governments also have three branches. The names of jobs may be different. For example, the leader of the United States is the president. The leader of a state government is the governor. The leader of a city may be the mayor. But each of these people is the leader of the executive branch of that government. Each leader has the job of carrying out the laws.

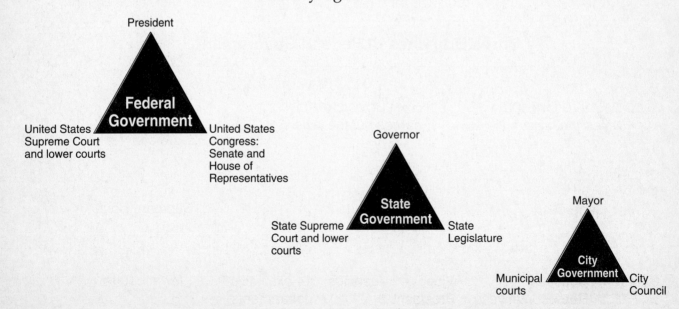

President

United States Supreme Court and lower courts

Federal Government

United States Congress: Senate and House of Representatives

Governor

State Supreme Court and lower courts

State Government

State Legislature

Mayor

Municipal courts

City Government

City Council

How Governments Work Together

Local, state, and federal governments have their own powers. Only the federal government can print money and stamps. Only the federal government can send the American army into war. Only the federal government can deal with other nations.

The states have different powers. Each state makes its own laws about the age for getting a driver's license. States pass their own traffic laws. State governments make many of the laws for public schools. Each state makes its own laws about marriage and divorce.

For example, in Utah a couple can get married with their parents' permission at age 14. In Oregon, couples need their parents' permission to marry at age 17. In some states couples need to have blood tests before they can get a marriage license. In some states couples have to wait a few days after they get their marriage license to get married.

Local, state, and federal governments have separate powers. But they also work together to provide services for your community.

Governments provide many services.

Compare the Federal Government and State Governments

Federal Government

1. President leads executive branch.
2. prints money
3. has U.S. Supreme Court
4. can send army into war
5. in Washington, D.C.

Both Kinds of Government

1. have constitutions
2. have three branches
3. pass tax laws
4. collect taxes
5. provide services

State Governments

1. Governor leads executive branch.
2. make public school laws
3. have state courts
4. pass marriage laws
5. in every state

State and local governments provide many of the services you need. They provide police and fire services. They collect garbage. They provide public hospitals and health services. They make laws about public schools and libraries. These governments provide public buses and trains. They also take care of parks and beaches.

Often the federal government passes laws that are carried out by state governments. For example, the federal government passed laws to have Head Start school programs for young children. The federal government gives each state money for these programs. Then each state decides on the kind of Head Start programs it wants to have.

Paying for Government

Local, state, and federal governments spend a lot of money. Programs like Head Start are expensive. Libraries, public schools, parks, and roads cost millions of dollars. Thousands of people work in government offices across the country. The federal government keeps an army, navy, and air force. Tax money pays for all of these services.

The federal government collects taxes. Most people who earn income in America pay income taxes to the federal government. People who have large incomes pay more income taxes than people with low incomes.

State and local governments also collect taxes. Many states have their own income tax laws. Many cities have their own income tax laws, too. For example, if you live in New York City, you have to pay income taxes to the city, state, and federal governments. It is against the law to refuse to pay income taxes. People who do not pay their income taxes can go to jail. Some states, like Texas, do not have city or state income taxes.

State and local governments also get money from sales taxes. A sales tax is a tax on most products sold in stores. Each state can decide how much sales tax to collect. A few states do not have sales taxes. Local governments can have their own sales taxes, too. State and local governments use sales tax money to pay for many kinds of services.

Your federal, state, and local governments have passed laws to protect your freedoms. Every day these governments provide services for millions of people across the nation.

THANK YOU FOR SHOPPING WITH US!

MAGAZINE	1.75
FACIAL TISSUE	.97
BUBBLEGUM	.50
MOUTHWASH	2.67
LIGHT BULB	.99
SUBTOTAL	6.88
8.00% TAX	.55
TOTAL	7.43

Some states collect money from sales taxes. This money helps pay for government services.

Writing Letters to Government Leaders

All Americans can write letters to their government leaders. You can write to leaders and legislators in federal, state, and local governments. Your letters will help leaders decide on the kinds of laws the country needs. Your letters help leaders learn what Americans need and want.

When you send a letter to a government leader, write neatly. Spell correctly. Put your address at the top of the page. Always sign your name. Put the correct mailing address and a stamp on your envelope.

You can use the addresses on this page to write to some of your federal leaders and legislators. When writing your letters, add the names of the leaders to the addresses.

The President of the United States
1600 Pennsylvania Avenue, NW
Washington, DC 20500

United States Senator
United States Senate
Washington, DC 20510

The Vice President of the United States
1600 Pennsylvania Avenue, NW
Washington, DC 20500

United States Representative
United States House of Representatives
Washington, DC 20515

Attorney General
Constitution Avenue & 10th Street, NW
Washington, DC 20530

Look at the letter on page 13. Donna Cole wrote the letter to the governor of Florida. She wanted Florida to have a tax on cigarettes. Donna also wrote letters about the cigarette tax to her state senator and representative.

▼▼▼

Use Donna's letter to answer the following questions.

1. Who was the governor of Florida in 1994? _____

2. What kind of tax does Donna want her state to have?

_____

12

3. What are two reasons Donna thinks this would be a good tax?

_____

_____

4. Donna wants to write a different letter to one of her representatives in Washington. What address can Donna use?

_____

_____

390 Lagoon Road
Miami, Florida 33139
March 2, 1994

Governor Lawton Chiles
Office of the Governor
The Capitol
Tallahassee, Florida 32399

Dear Governor Chiles:

Florida needs more money than it is now collecting from taxes. I think our state needs a cigarette tax.

People should pay a tax for each package of cigarettes that they buy. This tax will make cigarettes more expensive. More people will try to stop smoking.

The cigarette tax will also give our state more money to spend. It will help our state budget. I hope the cigarette tax becomes a law.

Sincerely,

Donna Cole

Donna Cole

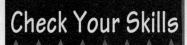

▶ **WORKSHOP PRACTICE: Write a Letter to a Government Leader**

The federal government needs more money than it now has.
It can get more money by raising taxes. Do you think
Congress should pass a law to raise income taxes or gasoline
taxes? On the lines below, write a letter to your United
States Senator. Tell the senator what kind of tax laws our
nation should or should not have. Explain your reasons. You
can rewrite your letter and mail it to Washington, D.C.

_____

_____

_____

_____

_____

_____

_____

_____

_____

_____

_____

_____

_____

_____

_____

_____

_____

COMPREHENSION: Circle the Answer
Draw a circle around the correct answer.

1. Which government controls the army and prints money?

federal   state   local

2. Which government makes laws about marriage, divorce, and driver's licenses?

federal   state   local

3. Which governments collect garbage and provide public libraries? (Circle two.)

federal   state   local

4. Which branch of government writes the laws?

legislative   executive   courts

5. What kind of taxes do people pay on the money they earn?

sales   school   income

 VOCABULARY: Matching
Match the word or phrase in Group B with a definition in Group A.
Write the letter of the correct answer on the line.

Group A	Group B
_____ **1.** This is a plan for government.	a. senators
_____ **2.** This is the government for the entire nation.	b. constitution
_____ **3.** Each state sends two of these legislators to the United States Senate.	c. federal
_____ **4.** This agency collects income taxes for the federal government.	d. executive
_____ **5.** This branch of government carries out the laws written by the legislative branch.	e. Internal Revenue Service

 **THINKING AND WRITING** In states that charge sales tax, all people must pay the same amount of tax on the products they buy. Do you think rich people and poor people should be charged the same sales tax? Explain your answer in your journal.

15

GOVERNMENT SERVICES

Think About As You Read

▶ What services do state and local governments provide?

▶ What government programs help people with low incomes?

▶ What are some services provided by the federal government?

Karen Parker began using government services as soon as she left for work in the morning. First, she walked her son to public school. Then she rode on a city bus to her job. Before starting her job, Karen stopped at a post office to buy stamps. After work, Karen visited her sick mother. Her mother was being cared for in a city hospital.

The government is part of your life every day. You depend on the government for many kinds of services.

You use government services every day.

Local governments provide services such as garbage collection.

Local and State Government Services

You use the services of your state and local governments every day. These governments collect garbage. They provide clean drinking water. They provide the money for public schools and libraries.

Your local government keeps many records. It keeps a record of every birth, death, marriage, and divorce. Very soon after birth, every child is given a **birth certificate**. Your local government prepares a death certificate for each person who dies.

Your state has programs to help you if your income is low. Low-income families with children under age 18 can receive money from the government twice a month. This program is called **Aid to Families with Dependent Children**, or **AFDC**. Families use this money to pay for food, clothing, housing, and medicine. People with low incomes can also receive food stamps to help them buy food. Every state also helps people with low incomes pay for medical care. This program is called **Medicaid**. It helps pay for doctor and hospital bills.

A **birth certificate** is a paper from your local government that has information about your name, birth, and parents.

Aid to Families with Dependent Children (AFDC) is a program that provides money to low-income families with children. The federal and state governments share the cost of this program.

Every state provides a **Medicaid** program to help people with low incomes pay for medical care. This program is paid for by the states and the federal government.

A **state employment agency** can help you find a job. You do not pay the agency for this service.

If you lose your job, your state's **unemployment insurance** program may pay part of your salary while you look for work.

Your state's **workers' compensation** program may pay part of your salary and medical bills if you get hurt or sick while working.

The federal government has passed laws that say states have to provide money, food stamps, and Medicaid to low-income families. Each state receives some money from the federal government for these programs. Then each state decides how to run these programs to meet the needs of the people in that state.

Your state also has programs to help workers. If you need a job, a **state employment agency** in your area may help you find one. These agencies receive money from the federal government.

Every state has a program called **unemployment insurance**. This program may pay part of your salary if you lose your job. If you lose your job, visit your state's unemployment office to find out if you can receive this kind of insurance.

Every state also has a program called **workers' compensation**. This program helps people who get hurt while working. You may be able to receive money from this program if you are hurt at your job.

Your state government provides a state employment agency to help you find a job.

A federal government agency helps people become United States citizens.

Federal Government Services

Every year many people move to the United States from other countries. These people need permission papers to live and work in the United States. This type of paper is called a green card. You can get a green card from a federal agency called **Immigration and Naturalization Services**, or **INS**. This agency has many offices throughout the country.

Immigration and Naturalization Services also helps people from other countries become **citizens** of the United States. An adult who is 18 years or older and has lived in this country for five years can try to become a citizen. To become a citizen, you have to complete INS forms and meet with an INS officer. After you become a citizen, you will have the same rights as a person who was born in this nation. The only difference is that you cannot become President or Vice President of the United States.

Immigration and Naturalization Services (INS) is a federal agency that helps people from other nations get legal papers to live in the United States. It also helps people become American citizens.

Citizens are members of a nation and have the rights of that nation.

EIGHT FEDERAL AGENCIES AND THEIR SERVICES

Agency	Services
Immigration and Naturalization Services	Helps people from other nations get green cards and become citizens
Food Safety and Inspection Service	Checks and grades meat, chicken, turkey, and dairy products
Social Security Administration	Provides social security income and medical insurance to older people and people with disabilities
Federal Bureau of Investigation (FBI)	Finds evidence about crimes for the federal government
Internal Revenue Service	Collects federal income taxes
Food and Drug Administration	Checks food and medicine for safety
Equal Employment Opportunity Commission	Carries out laws to end job discrimination
Food and Nutrition Service	Provides food stamps and school breakfast and lunch programs

The **Food and Drug Administration (FDA)** is a federal agency that checks the safety of foods, medicines, and make-up.

You use other services of the federal government. Federal agencies make all of the money used in this country. The federal government makes all stamps. It runs all post offices. The federal government also gives money to the states for job training programs. Through one of these programs, you may get a better job.

Most people who earn income have to pay taxes to the Internal Revenue Service, or IRS. This federal agency also has a program that helps people who work and have low incomes. This program is called Earned Income Tax Credit. If you are a worker with a low income, this program may help you pay less federal income tax. Then you can keep more of the money you earn. You may even receive money from the IRS. To learn more about this program, call an IRS office near your home.

Federal agencies help you in other ways. An agency called the **Food and Drug Administration**, or **FDA**, checks all new medicines. It makes sure that medicines really do what their companies say they will do. This agency does not allow unsafe medicines to be sold.

Another federal agency checks your food. The agency makes sure that meat, fish, and eggs are healthy and safe. Another agency gives money to states for food stamps. This agency also gives money to states for school breakfast and lunch programs.

Using Government Services

There are many government services that can help you. Many of these services are run by state and local governments. You can get information from your state and local governments about the services they provide. In many states you can get this information by calling the **department of social services**.

The **Department of Housing and Urban Development**, or **HUD**, is a federal agency that offers low-cost housing. HUD gives money to each state to help people with low incomes find housing. Some of this money is used to help people pay rent. Other money is used to pay for apartments in public housing. These apartments are in buildings that belong to the government. Some states use HUD money to give loans to people with low incomes. Then they can buy their own homes.

The government also provides you with a small income when you stop working after the age of 62. This income is called social security. If you die before age 62, the government may pay money to your children and your wife or husband. The amount of income depends on how many years you worked. It also depends on how much money you paid into the plan.

Federal, state, and local governments provide hundreds of services. Postage stamps, money, schools, and safe medicines are just some of the services you use. Government is part of your life every day.

The **department of social services** is an agency that helps people with disabilities, people with low incomes, and older adults get many kinds of services. In some states it may be called the department of human services.

The **Department of Housing and Urban Development (HUD)** is part of the federal government. It helps people with low incomes find housing that they can afford.

Getting a Copy of Your Birth Certificate

A birth certificate is a record of your birth. You may be asked to show your birth certificate to prove your age or date of birth. You have to have a birth certificate to get a social security card or a passport.

If you have lost your birth certificate, you can get a copy of it from your local government. Some local governments keep birth certificates and other records in a place called the vital records office. Find out where your local government keeps birth certificates and other records. Find out how much your government charges for a copy of your birth certificate.

You can get a copy of your birth certificate by writing a letter to the vital records office of the county where you were born. Include a check for the correct amount of money with your letter. Your letter needs to have the following information.

1. Your full name at birth.

2. Your date of birth.

3. The place of your birth. Include the town or county.

4. Your present home address.

5. Your father's full name.

6. Your mother's maiden name. (This is your mother's last name when she was born.)

7. The reason that you need a copy of the birth certificate.

Karen Parker needed a copy of her birth certificate. She wrote the letter on page 23 to get an official copy.

▼ ▼ ▼

Use Karen's letter to answer the following questions.

1. Why does Karen need a copy of her birth certificate? _____

2. Where was Karen born? _____

3. What maiden name did Karen's mother have? _____

4. What is the cost of a birth certificate in Little Rock? _____

170 West 11th Street
Little Rock, AR 72202
March 18, 1994

Vital Records Office
Department of Health
4815 W. Markham Street
Slot 44
Little Rock, AR 72205

To Whom It May Concern:

Please send me an official copy of my birth certificate. I need it
to get a passport. Here is the information you need.

My full name at birth: Karen Sue Jackson
My date of birth: October 17, 1961
My place of birth: Pulaski County
My father's name: David Sam Jackson
My mother's maiden name: Linda Butler
My home address: 170 West 11th Street, Little Rock, AR 72202

There is a $5 check in this envelope to pay for the cost of the
birth certificate. Please send it to me as soon as possible.

Thank you.

Sincerely,

Karen Parker

Karen Parker

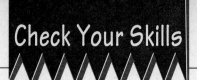

Check Your Skills

▶ **WORKSHOP PRACTICE:** Write a Letter for a Birth Certificate

On the lines below, write the information you would need to get a copy of your birth certificate. Then use the information to write a letter asking for a birth certificate. Write your letter on another sheet of paper.

1. County where you were born _____

2. Address of vital records office _____

_____

_____

3. Full name at birth _____

4. Date of birth _____

5. Place of birth _____

6. Father's full name _____

7. Mother's maiden name _____

8. Present address _____

▶ **COMPREHENSION:** True or False
Write True next to each sentence that is true. Write False next to each sentence that is false. There are two false sentences.

_____ **1.** The program called Aid to Families with Dependent Children gives money to low-income families with children.

_____ **2.** The federal government keeps records of births, deaths, marriages, and divorces.

_____ **3.** The INS is a federal agency that helps people from other nations get green cards and become citizens.

_____ **4.** Earned Income Tax Credit is a program that helps people with low incomes pay less taxes.

_____ **5.** Each state has an agency to make sure new medicines are safe.

On the lines that follow, rewrite the two false sentences to make them true.

_____

_____

_____

_____

VOCABULARY: Finish the Sentence

Choose one of the following words or phrases to complete each sentence. Write the word or phrase on the correct line.

citizens
Food and Drug Administration
Department of Housing and Urban Development
Medicaid
state employment agency
workers' compensation

1. Your state's _____ program helps people with low incomes pay for medical care.

2. Your _____ helps people find jobs and does not charge for its services.

3. Members of a nation are called _____ .

4. A person who gets sick or hurt from working at a job may get money called

_____ .

5. The _____ helps low-income people find housing that they can afford.

6. The _____ checks all new medicines.

THINKING AND WRITING Sometimes federal, state, and local governments try to save money by providing fewer services. Think about the agencies and services discussed in Chapter 2. Look at the chart on page 20 again. What services do you think the government could stop providing? Which ones are really necessary? In your journal explain how governments could save money.

THREE

KNOW YOUR RIGHTS

Think About As You Read

▶ What rights are protected in the Bill of Rights?

▶ What kinds of cases are decided in our court system?

▶ What are the rights of people who are arrested for crimes?

A natoly Karpov came to the United States from Romania. He left Romania because he wanted to live in a nation that allowed more freedom. The Romanian police had searched Anatoly's home without permission. His wife was arrested and sent to jail. After six months the police finally let her go. She never knew why she was arrested. She never had a **trial**. Anatoly felt lucky when he was able to move to the United States with his wife and son. He was glad to live in a nation where each person enjoys many kinds of rights.

A **trial** is an event where a person accused of a crime is judged in a court.

People from some other countries may come to the United States for more freedom.

Your rights allow you to have many freedoms. You can live where you choose. You can choose the kind of work you want to do. The laws of our nation protect your rights.

Your Constitutional Rights

The Constitution was written to protect the freedom of the American people. But it did not list the rights that the government must protect. Many people wanted the Constitution to promise that their rights would be protected. So the first ten **amendments** were added to the Constitution in 1791. These ten amendments are called the **Bill of Rights**. These amendments promise important rights to every person in the nation.

The Bill of Rights promises every person freedom of speech. This means you may say what you wish without being arrested. You will not be punished if you speak against the President and other government leaders.

The Bill of Rights promises freedom of religion to all. You may pray in the kind of church or temple you choose. You may go to church often or not at all. The government must be completely separate from religion. Public schools cannot teach religion to children.

The Bill of Rights promises freedom of the press. This means you may write what you wish in books, newspapers, and magazines. You cannot be arrested for writing ideas that government leaders dislike. But you are not allowed to write lies about other people.

The Bill of Rights protects people who are accused of crimes. You cannot be forced to speak against yourself. You must be treated fairly according to the law. You must be given a fair trial as quickly as possible. You cannot be held in jail for a long time without a trial. You have the right to have a lawyer defend your case. If you are found **guilty**, you must be given a fair punishment.

Amendments are laws that have been added to the Constitution.

The first ten amendments that were added to the Constitution are the **Bill of Rights**. These amendments protect your rights.

You are **guilty** if it is proven that you did a crime.

The Bill of Rights says that your state cannot pass laws that take away your rights. Your rights are protected. But you are not allowed to take away the rights and freedom of others.

Besides the Bill of Rights, other amendments have been passed. These amendments make sure your rights are protected. The Constitution was written over two hundred years ago. Amendments help the Constitution change with the times. One amendment says that all people must have equal protection under the law. This means you cannot be treated differently because of your sex, race, age, or disability. The chart below explains the rights and freedoms in the amendments to the Constitution.

Your Constitutional Rights

Constitutional Right	What the Right Means to You
Freedom of speech	You may say what you wish as long as you do not harm others.
Freedom of religion	You may pray the way you wish. You may also choose not to have a religion.
Freedom of the press	You may write what you wish in letters, books, newspapers, and magazines. You cannot write lies about other people.
Freedom of peaceful assembly	You may gather in groups to show how you feel about problems.
Freedom to petition	You may call, visit, or write to the President and other leaders about changes you want in government.
Right to be safe in your home	You have the right to be safe in your own home. Police must have a search warrant to search your home.
Right to fair treatment when accused of a crime	If you are accused of a crime, you must be treated fairly. You cannot be forced to speak against yourself.
Right to a fair trial	If you are accused of a crime, you have the right to a fair jury trial.
Right to equal protection under the law	The law must treat everyone equally. You cannot be treated differently because of your sex, race, religion, or disability.
Right to vote	The government cannot stop you from voting because of your sex or race. All citizens who are 18 and older can vote.

Your Rights and the Courts

The Constitution provides for courts. There are **criminal courts** and **civil courts**. People who are accused of breaking the law are tried in criminal courts. For example, people accused of a crime like murder are put on trial in criminal courts.

Civil courts decide how to solve problems between people. Usually no law has been broken. For example, a person who rents an apartment may have a problem with the landlord. That problem can be decided in a civil court. Civil courts may also hear problems about divorce, money, or accidents. If you and another person have a problem and cannot solve it, you may bring your problem to a civil court. A judge will decide how to solve the problem.

The Rights of Arrested People

The Constitution protects you from being arrested unfairly. The police can arrest a person that they see doing a crime. The police may not see a person **commit** a crime. But they can arrest a person if they have **evidence** that the person committed a crime.

Criminal courts decide if an accused person broke a law and committed a crime like murder or robbery.

Civil courts decide how to solve problems between people. Divorces are decided in civil courts.

To **commit** a crime means to do the crime.

Evidence is something that helps prove a person did a crime.

People cannot be treated differently because of their disabilities. All people have the right to freedom of peaceful assembly.

WARNING AS TO YOUR RIGHTS

You are under arrest. Before we ask you any questions, you must understand what your rights are.

You have the right to remain silent. You are not required to say anything to us at any time or to answer any questions. Anything you say can be used against you in court.

You have the right to talk to a lawyer for advice before we question you and to have him with you during questioning.

If you cannot afford a lawyer and want one, a lawyer will be provided for you.

If you want to answer questions now without a lawyer present you will still have the right to stop answering at any time. You also have the right to stop answering at any time until you talk to a lawyer.

The **Miranda warning** is the warning police must tell all people they arrest. It tells accused people of their rights.

A **jury** is a group of people who decide if an accused person is guilty of a crime.

Prejudiced people have bad ideas about others before knowing them.

The Constitution protects your rights if you are arrested. The police must read the **Miranda warning** to you if you are arrested. You have the right to be silent and not answer questions. A lawyer will be provided for you if you cannot pay for your own lawyer. If you decide to answer police questions, everything you tell the police can be used against you.

You have other rights if you are accused of a crime. You have the right to know why you have been arrested. You also have the right to know what evidence the police have against you. You are allowed one phone call. You may call a lawyer or another person who can help you.

After you are arrested, a court must quickly decide if there is enough evidence to keep you in jail while you wait for a trial. You must be allowed to go free if there is not enough evidence.

An accused person has a right to a trial by **jury**. The people who are picked to be on the jury cannot be **prejudiced** against you. You have the right to have a lawyer defend you at your trial.

You enjoy many kinds of rights. Accused people have rights, too. They cannot be punished until they are proven guilty. The Constitution was written to protect the rights and freedom of all Americans.

LIFE SKILLS Workshop

Filing a Claim in Small Claims Court

Small claims courts are civil courts. They are used to solve problems that do not involve very large amounts of money. Most of the time, a claim must be for less than $5,000. Each state has its own laws about how much money you can sue for. Each state also has its own rules about when, where, and how to file a claim in a small claims court. It does not cost much to bring your claim to a small claims court. You do not need a lawyer. You pay only a small fee to the court.

Follow these steps to have your claim heard in a small claims court.

1. Call the small claims court in your state to find out how and where to file a claim. Ask how you can get a form for filing a claim in court.

2. Complete the form for filing a claim. Find out whether you can take it or mail it to the court clerk. In some states you must sign the form in front of the clerk. Other states allow you to use a **notary**. A notary is someone who can stamp that the form was signed by you. Then you can mail the form to the court.

3. The person you are suing is the **defendant**. Decide how to let the defendant know about your claim. Sometimes the defendant decides to pay the amount of the claim without a trial. If the defendant does not want to pay, the defendant can ask for a trial.

4. Get a date for a trial. Prepare what you will say in court.

5. Go to court for your trial at the right time and date. Your trial will last only a few minutes. There will not be a jury. A judge will decide whether you win or lose.

6. If you win your case, collect the money the judge has told the defendant to pay you. The defendant will be given a certain amount of time to pay what is owed.

To bring your case to a small claims court, you must first complete a form. All states have their own forms, but they will be much like the form on page 33.

Completing a Small Claims Court Form

When Anatoly Karpov rented his apartment, he gave his landlord, Alice Dolan, a $700 deposit. When he moved out, he thought his apartment was clean and in good condition. He asked Dolan to return his deposit. She refused because the sink and stove needed repairs. Karpov did not want to lose his deposit. So he sued Dolan for $700 in small claims court. At the trial the judge said that Dolan's repairs might cost $150. The judge ordered Dolan to return $550 to Karpov. By going to small claims court, Karpov got back most of his deposit. Look at the small claims court form completed by Karpov on page 33. Notice the following parts.

1 ▶ **Information About the Plaintiff and the Defendant.** You are the **plaintiff** if you are the person who is bringing the case to court. The defendant is the person you are suing.

2 ▶ **Information About the Claim.** Write the amount of money you are suing for. Explain why you are bringing the case to court.

3 ▶ **Signatures.** You must have tried to collect the amount before filing a claim. Sign your name as the plaintiff. You must sign the form in the presence of a court clerk or a notary. The clerk or notary must sign the form. This part also lists the amount you pay to file the claim.

4 ▶ **Notice to Defendant.** The court clerk signs the form to show that it is a true copy. This form is shown to the defendant.

▼ ▼ ▼

Answer the following questions about filing a small claims court claim.

1. Who is the defendant on this claim? _____

2. Who is the plaintiff on this claim? _____

3. How much were Karpov's filing fees? _____

4. Do you need a lawyer in small claims court? _____

5. Who decides a case in small claims court? _____

IN THE DISTRICT COURT OF THE STATE OF OREGON
FOR THE COUNTY OF MARION
SMALL CLAIMS DEPARTMENT

PLEASE PRINT LEGIBLY

1

Anatoly Karpov

610 Lumber Road NE

Salem, Oregon 97305
Plaintiff

Address (include zip code)

555-5717
Telephone

vs.

Alice Dolan

893 Merry Street NE
Defendant

Salem, Oregon 97305

Address (include zip code)

555-9393
Telephone

No. _____

CLAIM AND NOTICE OF CLAIM

2

I, Plaintiff, claim that on or about **Feb. 1** , 19 **94** , the above named Defendant of **Marion** County, Oregon, owed me the sum of $ **700** , and this sum is still owing for **the deposit of 2 months rent for the apartment I rented from Alice Dolan.** .

3

STATE OF OREGON,)
) SS
COUNTY OF MARION,)

I, the above named plaintiff, having been duly sworn, state that I have read the above claim and that it is true as I verily believe, and that I have made a bona fide effort to collect the claim from the defendant before filing the claim with the Clerk.

Anatoly Karpov
Plaintiff

Subscribed and sworn to before me this **24** day of **Feb** , 19 **94** .

TRIAL COURT ADMINISTRATOR

(SEAL)

By: _____

Total filing fees and service expenses paid $ **54.10**

4

NOTICE TO DEFENDANT:
I certify that the foregoing is a true copy of a claim filed against you.

(SEAL)

By: _____

▶ **WORKSHOP PRACTICE: Complete a Small Claims Court Form**

Imagine that you took your winter coat to Freshway Cleaners to be cleaned. After your coat was cleaned, you found small holes all over it. You believe your coat was ruined by Freshway Cleaners. Freshway refuses to pay you the $150 that your coat cost. You decide to sue Freshway in small claims court. Freshway is at 1800 Main Street, Salem, Oregon 97301. It is in Marion County. The store phone number is 555-3313. Use this information to complete the form below.

**IN THE DISTRICT COURT OF THE STATE OF OREGON
FOR THE COUNTY OF MARION
SMALL CLAIMS DEPARTMENT**

PLEASE PRINT LEGIBLY

_____)
_____)
                                Plaintiff)   No. _____
_____)
Address (include zip code))
_____)   **CLAIM AND NOTICE OF CLAIM**
Telephone)
             vs.)
_____)
_____)
                      Defendant)
_____)
Address (include zip code))
_____)
Telephone

I, Plaintiff, claim that on or about _____ , 19 ____ , the above named Defendant of _____ County, Oregon, owed me the sum of $ _____ , and this sum is still owing for _____

_____ .

▶ **VOCABULARY: Find the Meaning**

On the line write the word or phrase that best completes each sentence.

1. Laws that have been added to the Constitution are called

_____ .

      bills   opinions   amendments

2. A court that decides if an accused person is guilty of a crime

is a _____ court.

criminal   civil   traffic

3. A _____ court solves problems between people.

criminal   civil   traffic

4. At a trial a group of people called the _____
decide if the accused person is guilty.

agency   Congress   jury

► COMPREHENSION: Write the Answer

Write one or more sentences to answer each question.

1. Why was the Bill of Rights added to the Constitution? _____

_____

_____

2. What does the Bill of Rights say about freedom of religion? _____

_____

_____

3. What does the "right to equal protection under the law" mean? _____

_____

_____

4. What does the Miranda warning mean? _____

_____

_____

THINKING AND WRITING Which rights and freedoms from the Constitution and Bill of Rights are most important to you? In your journal explain why you are glad that you have these rights.

DISCRIMINATION

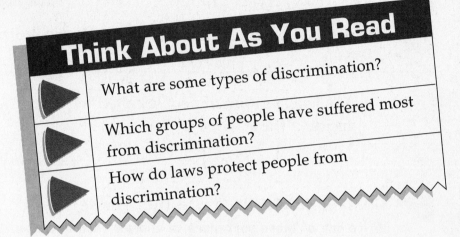

Think About As You Read

▸ What are some types of discrimination?

▸ Which groups of people have suffered most from discrimination?

▸ How do laws protect people from discrimination?

An **employer** is the person or business that hires you for a job.

Discrimination means treating people unfairly because of age, sex, race, religion, or disability.

Carmen Sanchez is deaf. She knows how to speak, but some people find it hard to understand her. Carmen worked as a typist for a few years. Then she tried to get a better-paying job as a typist for a different business. The **employer** did not hire Carmen. A different person who could not type as fast was hired instead. Carmen felt she did not get the job because of **discrimination** against workers who are disabled.

All people have the right to be treated fairly.

Workers cannot be forced to retire before age 70.

In this chapter you will read about discrimination. You will learn what you can do if someone **discriminates against** you.

Understanding Discrimination

Discrimination is the unfair treatment of people because they are different. People may be discriminated against because of their age, sex, or religion. They may be discriminated against because of their race or **disability**. Prejudiced people may discriminate against people who come to live in America from other countries.

Many people are hurt by job discrimination each year. This means you might not get hired because of your race, sex, age, religion, or disability. Another kind of job discrimination happens when you are paid less money for doing a job because of your age, race, or sex. Job discrimination also happens when you deserve a better job but you do not get it because of your sex, race, religion, or disability. Instead, the job is given to a person with less skill. Job discrimination is **illegal**.

To **discriminate against** someone means to treat that person unfairly.

A **disability** is a problem that makes a person less able to do certain things. If you have a hearing disability, then you do not hear very well.

Illegal means against the law.

37

Your **national origin**
is the country where
you were born.

Sexual harassment
is acts and words
about sex that make
you feel uncomfortable
on the job.

Minority groups are
groups of people in a
nation that are not like
most people in that
nation. For example,
the difference may be
race or religion.

People are also hurt by housing discrimination. This means you cannot buy or rent a home because of your race, religion, or **national origin**. Housing discrimination is also illegal.

Sexual harassment is another form of discrimination. Sexual harassment can be words or acts that make you feel uncomfortable on the job. Your employer may pressure you for a date. You may feel that you have to go on the date or you will not move up in the company. Both men and women employers can be guilty of sexual harassment. Sometimes sexual harassment is done by other workers in the company. Sexual harassment is illegal.

Who Has Suffered Most from Discrimination?

Discrimination has hurt many **minority groups**. Minority groups include Native Americans and Hispanics. African Americans and Asians have been discriminated against because of their race. Jews have faced discrimination because of their religion.

Women also face discrimination. They are sometimes paid less money than men for doing the same work. It is harder for women to become leaders in business and government.

People who are disabled face discrimination at work. Many employers do not want to hire them. They also face discrimination in public places. People who are blind cannot read the price labels in stores. People in wheelchairs have trouble finding stores, restaurants, hotels, and bathrooms where they can move around easily.

Laws That Fight Discrimination

The fourteenth amendment to the Constitution says the laws must give equal protection to all people. Because of this amendment, laws have been passed to fight discrimination.

Many stores and businesses are planning for the needs of people with disabilities.

The Civil Rights Act of 1964 was the first important law to fight discrimination. This law said that all people must be hired and fired fairly. It also said that all people have the right to use public places like restaurants, parks, and hotels.

Affirmative action programs were started because of the 1964 law. These programs help African Americans and other minority groups get better jobs. They also help people with disabilities. Many large companies now hire more women and more people from minority groups because of these programs.

Other laws have been passed to fight discrimination. Here are some ways these laws are working against discrimination.

1. Employers cannot discriminate when they hire and fire workers. They cannot discriminate when giving people better jobs.

2. Men and women must be paid the same money for doing the same work.

Affirmative action programs give a certain number of jobs to women, members of minority groups, and people with disabilities.

All students have the right to take part in classroom activities.

3. It is illegal to refuse to hire people because they are more than 40 years old. Workers cannot be forced to retire before the age of 70.

4. Labor unions cannot refuse to accept new members because of their age, race, sex, or disability.

5. All people have the right to live any place they can afford. It is illegal to refuse to sell or rent to a person from a minority group.

To **sue** means to take someone to court.

6. You have the right to **sue** people who discriminate against you.

7. Employers cannot discriminate against pregnant women. A woman cannot be forced to leave her job because she is pregnant.

Illegal aliens are people who come to the United States from other nations without the permission of the United States government.

8. Employers cannot refuse to hire people because of their national origin. But employers cannot hire **illegal aliens**.

9. Employers cannot refuse to hire people because of their religion. Workers cannot be forced to do activities that are against their religion.

40

10. Employers cannot refuse to hire people with disabilities who have the skills to do the job. Businesses have to try to make changes in their buildings to make it easier for people with disabilities to work there.

11. Every child who is disabled has the right to a public school education.

Discrimination laws do not protect workers who use illegal drugs. Employers can test their workers for drug abuse. They do not have to hire people who use illegal drugs. They can fire workers for using illegal drugs.

Carrying Out Laws Against Discrimination

Laws protect you from discrimination. Agencies carry out these laws. The **Equal Employment Opportunity Commission**, or **EEOC**, makes sure that laws against job discrimination are obeyed. This federal agency has offices in many states.

The EEOC can help you if you have suffered from job discrimination. Call the EEOC if you feel an employer discriminated against you. An EEOC worker will talk to you about your problem. You will be asked to fill out a form. Then EEOC workers will try to learn more about what happened. Employers can be punished if the EEOC proves that they have not obeyed discrimination laws.

Other agencies protect your right to fair housing. Perhaps you faced discrimination when buying or renting a home. Call the Human Rights Commission in your area. This agency will protect your housing rights.

Many laws have been passed that protect you from discrimination. You have the right to be treated fairly when you look for a home or a job. Government agencies can help you keep these important rights.

The **Equal Employment Opportunity Commission (EEOC)** is a federal agency that makes sure that laws against job discrimination are obeyed.

41

Filing a Discrimination Charge

If you have faced job discrimination, the EEOC can help you. Call the EEOC office nearest your home. An EEOC worker will ask you to explain how your employer discriminated against you. If the EEOC worker agrees that there was a problem, you will be sent a discrimination charge form. After the EEOC receives your completed form, workers there will check your story. An employer can be punished if the EEOC finds that the employer discriminated against you.

Carmen Sanchez felt that she was discriminated against because she is deaf. Notice the following parts of Carmen's discrimination form.

1 **State or Local Agency.** If you are discriminated against at your job, report to the employment office at your job first. If no one helps you fill out this form, then call your state or local human rights office. If a company does not hire you because of discrimination, call your state human rights office or the EEOC office nearest you.

2 **Who Discriminated Against You.** You may list more than one person, group, or company that discriminated against you.

3 **Cause of Discrimination.** "Retaliation" means someone is trying to get even with you, perhaps for reporting illegal acts at your job. "Other" may include sexual harassment.

▼ ▼ ▼

Answer these questions about Carmen's completed form.

1. Which employer is this charge against? _____

2. What kind of job did Carmen want? _____

3. How fast can Carmen type? _____

4. How fast can the person who was hired type? _____

5. Why does Carmen feel that she has been discriminated against?

_____

CHARGE OF DISCRIMINATION

This form is affected by the Privacy Act of 1974; see Privacy Act Statement on reverse before completing this form.

ENTER CHARGE NUMBER
☐ FEPA
☐ EEOC

1 State of Illinois Human Rights Commission ____ and EEOC
(State or Local Agency, if any)

NAME *(Indicate Mr. (Ms.) or Mrs.)*　Carmen Sanchez

HOME TELEPHONE NO. *(Include Area Code)*　312-555-1907

STREET ADDRESS　CITY, STATE AND ZIP CODE
124 Montrose Avenue West Chicago, IL 60613

COUNTY　Cook

2 NAMED IS THE EMPLOYER, LABOR ORGANIZATION, EMPLOYMENT AGENCY, APPRENTICESHIP COMMITTEE, STATE OR LOCAL GOVERNMENT AGENCY WHO DISCRIMINATED AGAINST ME *(If more than one, list below.)*

NAME　Smith's Box Company

NO. OF EMPLOYEES/MEMBERS　35

TELEPHONE NUMBER *(Include Area Code)*　312-555-6302

STREET ADDRESS　25 Birch Avenue South

CITY, STATE AND ZIP CODE　Chicago, IL 60617

NAME

TELEPHONE NUMBER *(Include Area Code)*

STREET ADDRESS

CITY, STATE AND ZIP CODE

3 CAUSE OF DISCRIMINATION BASED ON *(Check appropriate box(es))*
☐ RACE　☐ COLOR　☐ SEX　☐ RELIGION　☐ NATIONAL ORIGIN
☐ AGE　☐ RETALIATION　☑ OTHER *(Specify)* disability

DATE MOST RECENT OR CONTINUING DISCRIMINATION TOOK PLACE *(Month, day, year)*
Jan. 10, 1994

THE PARTICULARS ARE *(If additional space is needed, attach extra sheet(s)):*

I applied for a typing job at Smith's Box Company. I can type 65 words a minute, and I had a good job recommendation from my last typing job. Mr. Smith told me I could not have the job because he needed a better typist. Then I learned from a friend who works for Mr. Smith that he hired a different typist who types only 50 words a minute. I feel I didn't get the job because Mr. Smith did not want a deaf typist. He hired a hearing person who does not type as well as I do.

☑ I also want this charge filed with the EEOC. I will advise the agencies if I change my address or telephone number and I will cooperate fully with them in the processing of my charge in accordance with their procedures.

NOTARY - (When necessary to meet State and Local Requirements)

I swear or affirm that I have read the above charge and that it is true to the best of my knowledge, information and belief.

I declare under penalty of perjury that the foregoing is true and correct.

SIGNATURE OF COMPLAINANT

SUBSCRIBED AND SWORN TO BEFORE ME THIS DATE *(Day, month, and year)*

Feb. 11, 1994　Carmen Sanchez
Date　Charging Party *(Signature)*

WORKSHOP PRACTICE: File a Discrimination Charge

Read this paragraph about discrimination.

> Janet Wilson worked at the All Star Company for one year. She was the company's only woman worker. She always finished all of her work each day. On February 7, her employer fired her for being a slow worker. The employer hired a male worker for the job. Janet felt that she was fired for unfair reasons. She decided to file a Charge of Discrimination with the EEOC.

Imagine that you are Janet Wilson. Complete this part of the discrimination charge form. Use it to explain why you felt you were discriminated against.

CHARGE OF DISCRIMINATION

CAUSE OF DISCRIMINATION BASED ON *(Check appropriate box(es))* ☐RACE ☐COLOR ☐SEX ☐RELIGION ☐NATIONAL ORIGIN ☐AGE ☐RETALIATION ☐OTHER *(Specify)*	DATE MOST RECENT OR CONTINUING DISCRIMINATION TOOK PLACE *(Month, day, year)*
THE PARTICULARS ARE *(If additional space is needed, attach extra sheet(s))*:	

VOCABULARY: Writing with Vocabulary Words
Use five or more of the following words or phrases to write a paragraph that tells about discrimination.

discrimination
employers
sue
EEOC
sexual harassment
minority groups
illegal

_____

_____

_____

_____

_____

_____

COMPREHENSION: Finish the Paragraph
Use the following words or phrases to finish the paragraph. Write the words you choose on the correct lines.

Civil Rights Act
disability
housing
job
national origin
pregnant

People may face discrimination because of their age, race, sex, religion, _____ , or _____ . People may face _____ discrimination from employers. An employer cannot refuse to hire a _____ woman. People may face _____ discrimination when they want to buy or rent a home. The first important law to end discrimination was the _____ of 1964.

THINKING AND WRITING Have you or someone you know been hurt by discrimination? If not, imagine that you have. In your journal explain what happened and what actions could be taken against this type of discrimination.

FIVE

GETTING A DRIVER'S LICENSE

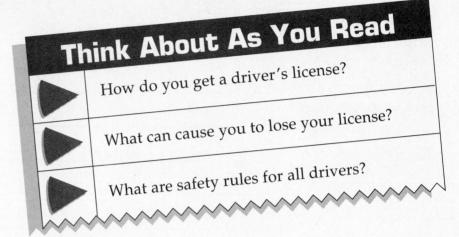

Think About As You Read

▶ How do you get a driver's license?

▶ What can cause you to lose your license?

▶ What are safety rules for all drivers?

Jim Reed has a new job. He enjoys his work, and he is earning more money. But this new job is farther from his home. Jim finds it hard to take three buses to work each day. It would be easier for Jim to get to work if he could drive his own car. Jim has decided to get a driver's license. Then he will buy a car for himself. In this chapter you will learn how to get a driver's license.

Getting to work on time is important.

Apply for a driver's license at the motor vehicle department in your state.

Preparing to Get a Driver's License

Each state has its own rules for driving a car and getting a license. You can learn these rules from the **motor vehicle department** in your state.

To get a license, study the driver's manual from your state's motor vehicle department. Learn the traffic laws from the manual. Learn how to read traffic signs. Learning the information in the manual is your first step for getting a driver's license.

After studying the driver's manual, go to the nearest office of the motor vehicle department. Fill out an **application** for a license. Pay your state's **fee** for the application. Take an eye test. Then take a written test. The written test asks you questions about traffic signs and driving rules. You have to pass the eye test and the written test before you can get a license.

In most states you will get a **learner's permit** after you pass the eye test and the written test. The permit allows you to practice driving if you have an experienced driver in the front seat of the car with you. You cannot drive alone with a learner's permit.

The **motor vehicle department** is the agency in your state that helps people get driver's licenses. It carries out traffic laws.

An **application** is a written form that is used to get permission to do something. Complete an application for a driver's license to get permission to learn to drive.

A **fee** is the money you pay for a service.

A **learner's permit** is a paper that gives you permission to practice driving before you get your driver's license.

47

How to Get a Driver's License

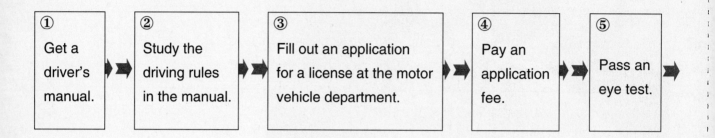

① Get a driver's manual.

② Study the driving rules in the manual.

③ Fill out an application for a license at the motor vehicle department.

④ Pay an application fee.

⑤ Pass an eye test.

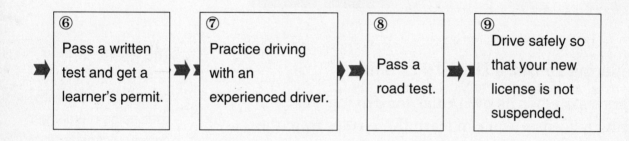

⑥ Pass a written test and get a learner's permit.

⑦ Practice driving with an experienced driver.

⑧ Pass a road test.

⑨ Drive safely so that your new license is not suspended.

Your **registration** for a car can be a card, paper, or sticker from your state's motor vehicle department that shows you own the car.

A license or car registration is **renewed** so it can continue to be used for a certain period of time.

Practice driving after you get a permit. You may want to take lessons with a teacher from a driver education program. After you feel you have had enough practice, set up a time to take a driving test at the motor vehicle department. You will get a driver's license after you pass this test.

After you get a license, you can think about owning a car. Your car has to be registered with your state's motor vehicle department. Pay fees to register your car and to receive license plates for your car. The **registration** has to be **renewed** every year or every few years. Many states require owners to have car insurance in order to register their cars. Every driver needs insurance.

If you move from one state to another, find out how to get a driver's license in your new state. Each state has its own rules about giving licenses to drivers who move from other states. If you have a license from another state, you will probably have to pass an eye test and a written test in your new state. You may also have to pass a driving test. Your car will have to be registered in your new state, too. Call the motor vehicle department in your new state to learn what to do. In some states you must get your new license within 30 days after you move.

Always drive a car that is safe. Your car needs good tires and brakes. Keep a spare tire in your car. Your car needs working headlights and taillights. Make sure the **turn signals** work. Your car needs to be checked for safety at least once a year. Many states require cars to pass a **safety inspection** when drivers renew their registration.

Keeping Your Driver's License

A driver's license has to be renewed every three to five years. In most states you have to pay a fee and pass an eye test to renew your license. Most of the time, you do not take a written test or a road test again. Renew your license before it **expires**. You cannot drive with an expired license.

Unsafe drivers can lose their licenses. The police watch for drivers who break traffic laws. Breaking a traffic law is called a **violation**. Violations can be put on your record by the police. Your license can be **suspended** if you have too many violations in a short period of time. If you commit dangerous violations, your license can be **revoked**.

You can be sent to jail or forced to pay a fine if you drive after your license has been revoked. After a certain number of months or years have passed, you may be allowed to get a new license. You will have to pass the eye test, the written test, and the road test again.

The **turn signals** on your car are flashing lights that are used to show other drivers when you are making a left or right turn.

During a **safety inspection**, a person checks your car for safety. Many states will not allow you to register your car unless it has passed a safety inspection.

When a license or registration **expires**, it has come to the end of the period of time when it can be used.

Breaking a driving law is a **violation**.

A **suspended** license cannot be used for a certain period of time.

A **revoked** license can never be used again. A person no longer has the right to drive after a license has been revoked.

Do not pass a stopped school bus.

Four Serious Violations

You can lose your license for four kinds of violations.

1. Speeding is a violation. Obey the speed limit signs. Do not drive too fast.

2. Another violation is passing a stopped school bus when children are getting on or off. Do not pass a school bus if its red lights are flashing. Do not pass if the school bus has put out its red stop sign. The flashing lights and the red stop sign mean children are getting on or off. All cars that are traveling in the same direction as the school bus have to stop. In many states cars that are traveling on the opposite side of the road also have to stop. Learn the rules about stopped school buses for your state.

3. It is a violation to leave the scene of a car accident where people have been hurt or killed. If you are in an accident, stop and stay there until the police come. You will have to give the police information about the accident. The Life Skills Workshop on pages 53–54 tells you what to do if you are in a car accident.

4. It is a violation to drink alcohol and drive. This is called **driving while intoxicated**, or **DWI**. Alcohol makes you think and act more slowly. More than half of all car accidents are caused by drivers who have been drinking alcohol. Just one alcoholic drink can slow your thinking and can cause you to have an accident. Wait a few hours to drive if you have had an alcoholic drink. In every state police can stop you if they think you have been drinking. The police can ask you to take a breath test that can prove if you have been drinking alcohol. Your license can be suspended if you refuse to take the test.

Every state has tough laws to punish drivers who are driving while intoxicated. In some states you can be sent to jail immediately if you are found to be DWI. There are other punishments, too. Your license can be revoked. You may have to pay thousands of dollars in fines. Drivers who are caught drinking and driving more than once may be sent to jail. They may never be allowed to get a driver's license again.

Driving while intoxicated (DWI) means a driver has been drinking alcohol. A breath test will show if a driver has been drinking.

A breath test can show if a driver has been drinking alcohol.

51

Driving under the influence (DUI) means a driver has been drinking alcohol or using drugs. It is illegal.

It is also against the law to use drugs and drive. Do not take medicine that can make you sleepy if you plan to drive. Using alcohol and medicine together can be dangerous. In some states the violation is called **driving under the influence**, or **DUI**. This means you have been using alcohol or drugs.

Being a Safe Driver

Every year thousands of people are hurt in car accidents. You can avoid most accidents by following these safety rules.

1. Avoid driving if you are tired or upset.

2. Concentrate on driving. Try not to think about anything else.

3. Always leave plenty of space between your car and the cars in front and in back of you. Allow much more space when driving at a high speed. This space allows you room to stop if you have to. It also allows you to change lanes safely.

4. Drive at a safe speed. Do not go too fast or too slow. Drive slower in rain, snow, and fog. Drive very slow on icy roads. Drive slower at night.

5. Always wear a seat belt. Keep the shoulder strap over your shoulder. Tell all passengers to wear seat belts, too.

6. Never drive after drinking alcohol or using drugs.

Driving a car may help you get to work and visit family and friends. Always drive safely. By getting your driver's license, you will enjoy new freedom and new responsibility.

What to Do in Case of Accident

Safe drivers have fewer accidents. But sometimes even the best drivers are in car accidents. It is important to know what to do. Follow these twelve rules if you are in an accident.

1. Stop! Do not leave the place where the accident took place. In some states you can move your car to the side of the road so that you do not stop traffic.

2. Turn on your emergency flashing lights.

3. Check to see if anyone has been hurt in the accident. Cover the injured person with a blanket or coat.

4. Call the police. If a person has been injured, call an ambulance and a rescue team.

5. Exchange information with the drivers of the other cars. You need the name, address, and phone number of each driver and each passenger. Get the vehicle registration numbers and license plate numbers. You need the make, model, year, and color for each car.

6. Get insurance information from each driver. You need each driver's policy number and the name of the insurance company.

7. Do not fight or argue with the other drivers at the scene of the accident.

8. Sometimes other people have seen the accident. These people are **witnesses**. Get the names, addresses, and phone numbers of all witnesses.

9. While you are waiting for the police, write down what happened. Include the time, date, and place. Write down the direction that the cars were moving in. Include the weather and road conditions. Draw a picture or diagram that shows what happened at the accident.

10. The police will write a report about the accident. Ask the police to check that the information you wrote about the accident is correct.

11 Many car accidents cause damage to cars and property. They also injure and sometimes kill people. These accidents must be reported to the state motor vehicle department. They must also be reported to your insurance company.

12 If you hit an empty parked car, leave your name, address, phone number, and license number on that car's windshield. Report the accident to the police. Tell your insurance company what happened.

▼ ▼ ▼

Study the twelve rules about what to do if you are in a car accident. Answer the following questions.

1. What is the first thing you should do if you are in a car accident?

_____

_____

2. What do you need to do if a person has been hurt?

_____

_____

3. What information do you need to exchange with the other drivers?

_____

_____

4. What kinds of accidents need to be reported to the state motor vehicle department and to your insurance company?

_____

_____

5. What do you need to do if you hit an empty parked car?

_____

_____

_____

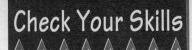

▶ **WORKSHOP PRACTICE: After a Car Accident**

Jim Reed was in a car accident while he was driving on a highway. Read the paragraph about Jim's accident. Then write a paragraph that tells all the things Jim has to do to take care of the accident correctly. Use the rules in the Life Skills Workshop on pages 53–54 to help you.

> Jim Reed was driving on a highway on a rainy day. A dog ran across the highway. The red car in front of Jim stopped suddenly to avoid hitting the dog. Jim tried to stop, but he could not stop in time. He crashed into the back of the red car. Both cars stopped and pulled over to the side of the road. Jim saw that the red car was badly damaged. Its driver's head was bleeding. Jim's neck hurt, and the front of his car was damaged.

_____

_____

_____

_____

_____

_____

_____

_____

_____

▶ **COMPREHENSION: True or False**

Write True next to each sentence that is true. Write False next to each sentence that is false. There are two false sentences.

_____ **1.** People need to avoid driving when they are very upset or tired.

_____ **2.** After you move to a new state, you can use your driver's license from your old state for a few years.

_____ **3.** Your license can be suspended or revoked if you get too many violations.

_____ **4.** Drivers are allowed to pass a stopped school bus when children are getting on and off.

_____ **5.** Driving while intoxicated or using drugs is a serious violation.

On the lines that follow, rewrite the two false sentences to make them true.

_____

_____

_____

 ## VOCABULARY: Finish the Sentence
Choose one of the following words or phrases to complete each sentence. Write the word or phrase on the correct line.

driving while
   intoxicated
revoked
suspended
registration
expired

1. A _____ license cannot be used for a certain period of time.

2. A _____ license can never be used again.

3. A person who is _____ has been drinking alcohol before or while driving.

4. Your _____ for a car is a paper, card, or sticker from the motor vehicle department that shows you own the car.

5. When a license or registration has _____ , it has come to the end of the period when it can be used.

 **THINKING AND WRITING** What are the most important things a person can do to be a safe driver? What are five rules for safe driving? In your journal explain why each of the rules you picked is important for safety.

TRAFFIC LAWS

Think About As You Read

▶ What are the laws about seat belts and stop signs?

▶ What parking rules do you need to know?

▶ What are the rules about who has the right of way?

Brian Cates was in a hurry. He had to stop at the drugstore to buy medicine for his sick child before going to work. Brian could not find a parking place near the drugstore. So he parked his car in front of a **fire hydrant**. When Brian returned to his car, he saw a parking ticket on his **windshield**. Brian had broken a traffic law by parking in front of a hydrant.

Drivers have to obey many traffic laws. You will learn more about these laws in this chapter.

A **fire hydrant** is a pump that is used to provide water to fight fires. Firefighters attach fire hoses to hydrants.

A **windshield** is the front window of a car or a truck.

It is illegal to park by a fire hydrant.

Traffic Safety Laws

All states require drivers to wear seat belts. State laws also require passengers in the front seat to wear seat belts. The other passengers in a car need to wear seat belts, too.

All states require small children to ride in special safety car seats. Each state has its own rules about the ages when children have to ride in safety car seats. These seats need to be attached to the car correctly with seat belts.

An **intersection** is where two streets cross each other.

In all states a stop sign means you have to come to a full stop. Sometimes your car may be the only vehicle at an **intersection** with a stop sign. You still have to come to a complete stop before you enter the intersection.

A **solid** line is a line without any breaks.

In every state white and yellow lines are painted on the roads. The laws about road lines are the same everywhere. You can pass from one lane to another when there is a broken white line. Cross a **solid** line only if it is necessary. Never cross a solid double line. Sometimes a broken line is next to a solid line. You can cross these lines only if you are driving on the side with the broken line.

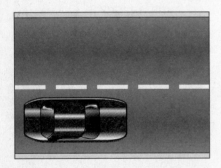

A broken line means you can pass from one lane to another.

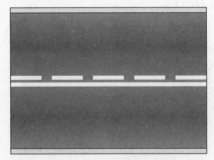

A broken line on your side of a solid line means you are allowed to pass. A solid line on your side means you are not allowed to pass.

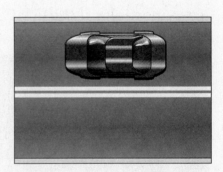

A solid double line means you cannot cross it.

All states require drivers to use headlights at night. Use headlights from the time the sun sets in the evening until it begins to rise in the morning. Some states require headlights on rainy days. Do not use your bright lights unless you are driving on dark country roads.

Some traffic laws differ from state to state. Each state has its own laws about driving while wearing headsets. It may be against the law for drivers in your state to wear headsets. It may be against the law in your state to have stickers on your windshields. Each state has its own rules about allowing dark **tinted** glass windows.

Tinted windows are coated to make them darker.

States have different laws for allowing drivers to make turns on red lights. Sometimes a local government has its own laws. In New York City, you are never allowed to make a turn on a red light. In other parts of New York state, drivers can make a right turn on a red light. But first they have to make a full stop and check the intersection for traffic. Learn your state's rules for making turns when the light is red.

Always wear seat belts.

Traffic Signs

Traffic signs are the same in every state. Study the signs below. Learn what each sign means.

Right Lane Ends
Merge left.

Yield
Slow down or stop to yield right of way.

Traffic Signal Ahead

Pedestrian Crossing
Watch for people crossing the street.

Railroad Crossing

Divided Highway Ends

T-Intersection
Turn right or left.

Deer/Animal Crossing
Watch for animals crossing suddenly.

One-Way Traffic
Do not enter road.

Railroad Crossing
Stop completely while train passes. Cross tracks carefully.

Two-Way Traffic

Winding Road

Slippery When Wet
Slow down on wet road.

Speed Limit
Do not drive faster than 55 miles per hour or less than 40.

Keep Right of Divider

Merging Traffic Entering from Right

Curve Ahead
Slow down for curve.

School Crossing
Slow down during school hours. Watch for children.

No U-Turn

One-Way Traffic
Do not enter road.

Hill Ahead

Right Turn Ahead
Slow down for turn.

No Left Turn

No Right Turn

Stop
Come to a complete stop.

On every roadway you will see signs that tell you the speed limit. Do not drive faster than that speed. More accidents happen when people drive faster than 55 miles an hour. Sometimes a speed sign will tell you a **minimum speed**. Do not drive slower than that speed.

When driving on a highway, you may need to pass another vehicle. Always try to use the left lane to pass. Learn your state's rules for using the right lane to pass.

Use turn signals when you change lanes, pass, and make turns. Sometimes your turn signals may not work. Then put your arm out the driver's window and use hand signals. The pictures below show the hand signals for turning left, turning right, and stopping.

The **minimum speed** is the slowest speed at which you are allowed to drive.

Parking Laws

There are some places where you are never allowed to park.

1. Never park in front of a fire hydrant. Park at least 15 feet in front of or in back of a hydrant.

Hand Signals

Left Turn

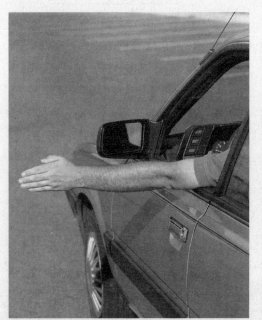

Right Turn

Stop

A **crosswalk** is an area in an intersection that is marked with lines. People walk across the street at this marked area.

To **double park** means to park to the left of cars that are already in the parking lane. It is against the law to double park.

2. Never park in a space that is for disabled drivers if you do not have a special license plate or sticker. These parking spaces have special signs.

3. Never park on a highway, bridge, or in a tunnel.

4. Never park on a sidewalk or in front of a driveway. You can get a ticket even if the driveway belongs to your own house.

5. Never park at a bus stop or on train tracks.

6. Never park where a sign says "No Parking" or "No Stopping at Any Time."

7. Never park on a **crosswalk**.

8. Never **double park**.

Pay attention to parking signs when you want to park. There may be days of the week or hours in the day when you cannot park on certain streets. A police officer can give you a parking ticket if you disobey parking rules. You pay a fine for each ticket.

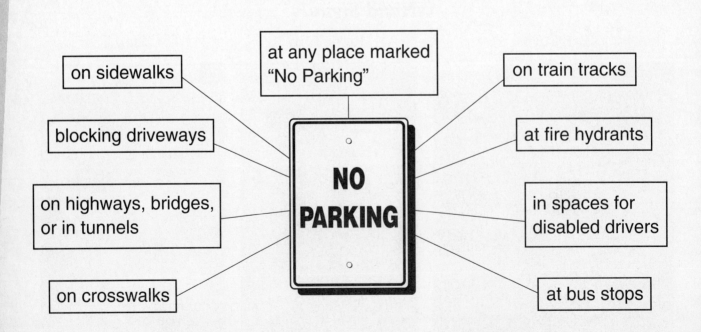

on sidewalks

at any place marked "No Parking"

on train tracks

blocking driveways

at fire hydrants

on highways, bridges, or in tunnels

NO PARKING

in spaces for disabled drivers

on crosswalks

at bus stops

Right-of-Way Laws

Right-of-way laws help prevent accidents. A right-of-way law tells which vehicle or person can move first when there is more than one vehicle or person at an intersection. When you do not have the right of way, always **yield** and allow the other vehicle to move ahead of you.

Follow these right-of-way rules.

1. Ambulances, fire trucks, and police cars with flashing red lights always have the right of way. Allow them to move ahead of you.

2. Always yield to a person who is crossing the street.

3. Yield to the vehicle that gets to the intersection first.

4. Yield to a vehicle that is already in the intersection.

5. Yield to a passing train.

6. When entering a highway, yield to the vehicles that are already on the highway.

Traffic laws protect drivers, passengers, and **pedestrians**. Obeying traffic laws will help you get where you want to go safely.

A vehicle or person that has the **right of way** can enter the highway or road before other vehicles or people.

To **yield** means to allow another person or vehicle to enter the road or highway before you.

A **pedestrian** is a person who walks.

Cars must stop for pedestrians in a crosswalk.

Paying a Traffic Fine

Brian Cates received a parking ticket because he parked in front of a fire hydrant. Look at Brian's ticket on page 65. Notice the following parts.

1 **Information About the Car and Driver.** The police officer did not fill out information about the driver because Brian was not in his car at the time.

2 **Traffic Court.** This part tells when and where you can go to have your case heard in traffic court. You go to traffic court if you feel you are not guilty of the violation. Then you can tell a judge why you are not guilty. The judge will decide if you have to pay the ticket.

3 **Pleading Guilty.** If you sign on this line on the back of the ticket, you are agreeing that you are guilty of the violation. You do not have to go to traffic court. You can mail in your payment. Your payment is due by the time of your court date.

4 **List of Violations and Fines.** Look at the list of violations to find out how much you have to pay. Brian circled his violation. Write a check or get a money order for that amount. Never send cash. Mail your check or money order to the traffic court.

▼ ▼ ▼

Answer the following questions about Brian's parking ticket.

1. What kind of car did Brian drive? _____

2. What day does Brian have to appear in Central Traffic Court if he feels he is not guilty? _____

3. To whom does Brian have to make his check? _____

4. When is Brian's payment due? _____

5. How much is Brian's fine? _____

POLICE DEPARTMENT, COUNTY OF NASSAU, N.Y.
PARKING TICKET

T560414

SERIAL NO.	INDEX NO.

SAMPLE

The People of the State of New York - Vs.
The Operator or Registered Owner of Vehicle Described Below

▶ 1

PLATE NUMBER	ABC 123		STATE	NY

VEHICLE: YEAR	MAKE	BODY TYPE	COLOR
1988	Ford	4door	white

DRIVER'S: LAST NAME	FIRST NAME	INITIAL	DATE OF BIRTH

DRIVER'S ADDRESS

DRIVER'S LICENSE NO.		STATE

CLASS	LICENSE EXPIRATION DATE	SEX ☐ MALE ☐ FEMALE	OPERATOR OWNS VEHICLE ☐ YES ☐ NO

You are Hereby Directed to Appear in The

▶ 2

☒ Central Traffic Court, 99 Main Street, Hempstead, New York 11550

☐ Other Court: NAME _____

ADDRESS _____

DATE OF APPEARANCE
ON THE **14** DAY OF **March** 19**94** AT **9:00** ☒ AM ☐ PM

To Answer a Charge in Violation of

SECTION	1202	SUBD	A3B	OF ☒ V.T.L. ☐ ORDINANCE ☐ OTHER (Specify)

OF ☒ N.Y.S. ☐ T.N.H. ☐ T.O.B. ☐ N.C. ☐ T.O.H. ☐ VILL. OF

☐ PARKED OVERTIME	HOURS AND	MINUTES IN A	HOUR ZONE	☐ PROHIBITED PARKING
☐ RESTRICTED PARKING	☐ PARKED BLOCKING DRIVEWAY	☐ INSPECTION VIOLATION	EXP. DATE	
☐ DOUBLE PARKED	☐ LOADING ZONE	☐ NO PARKING PERMIT	☐ EXPIRED METER	METER NO.
☒ BLOCKING A FIRE HYDRANT	☐ HANDICAPPED PARKING	☐ REGISTRATION VIOLATION	EXP. DATE	

SPECIFIC CHARGE

At Location

PLACE OF OCCURRENCE
300 Rose Street

HAMLET/VILLAGE	Oceanside	INC. VILL. ☐ YES ☒ NO

COUNTY	STATE	DATE	TIME	
NASSAU	N.Y.	2/8/94	10:50	☒ AM ☐ PM

ANY FALSE STATEMENTS MADE HEREIN ARE PUNISHABLE AS A CLASS A MISDEMEANOR PURSUANT TO SECTION 210.45 OF THE PENAL LAW.

RANK	OFFICER'S SIGNATURE	DATE
captain	Michael Jones	2/8/94

OFFICER'S NAME PRINTED	SHIELD NO.	SERIAL NO.	COMMAND
Michael Jones	8887	8979	9

A plea of Guilty to this charge is equivalent to a conviction after trial. If you are convicted, not only will you be liable to a penalty, but in addition, your license to drive a motor vehicle or motor-cycle, and your Certification of Registration, if any, are subject to suspension and revocation as prescribed by law.

TRAFFIC TICKET

THE FOLLOWING INSTRUCTIONS APPLY ONLY IF YOUR TICKET IS RETURNABLE AT THE CENTRAL TRAFFIC COURT, 99 MAIN STREET, HEMPSTEAD, N.Y. 11550

If you wish to plead guilty, you may do so by signing your name and address and paying the prescribed fine by either mailing the ticket or the fine to the court at the address shown above or by appearing personally at the court on any weekday between 9 A.M. and 4 P.M. Checks should be made payable to the "Clerk of the Court." Do not mail cash, car registration or operator's license. Fines must be paid by the return date shown on your ticket.

▶ 3

I PLEAD GUILTY _**Brian Cates**_
SIGNATURE
**9030 Oceanside Road**
ADDRESS
**Oceanside, NY 11572**

NOTE: Abandoning a motor vehicle on highway or other public property **must** be answered in person.
Fine schedule is applicable only if timely payment is made.

Violations for Which the Prescribed Fine is $50.00
1. Parking in a space reserved for the handicapped without a valid permit.
2. Uninspected motor vehicle – includes inspection sticker expired more than 60 days.
3. Unregistered motor vehicle – includes registration expired more than 60 days.

Violations for Which the Prescribed Fine is $25.00
1. Parking or abandoning a motor vehicle on a snow emergency route.
2. Uninspected motor vehicle – inspection sticker not more than 60 days past expiration date.
3. Unregistered motor vehicle – registration not more than 60 days past expiration of prior registration.
4. Parked in front of a fire hydrant.
5. Double parked.
6. Number plate violations – V.T.L. sections 402 and 412.

Violations for Which the Prescribed Fine is $15.00
1. All other parking offenses not listed above.

▶ 4

NOT GUILTY PLEAS
If you wish to plead not guilty, you may do so by appearing personally or mailing the ticket and a statement signed by you stating your desire to plead not guilty to the court where the ticket is returnable, such mailing to be by first class mail or by registered or certified mail, return receipt requested, within 48 hours after receipt of the ticket by you. **If you plead not guilty, you will be required to appear personally at court for trial on a date set by the court.**

IF RETURNABLE IN OTHER THAN CENTRAL TRAFFIC COURT

This ticket is returnable in the _____

Court, located at _____

_____, New York. The fine for the offense shown can be ascertained by contacting the court. If the fine is to be mailed, the fine and the ticket must be sent to the clerk of the above court on or before the return date. **Do not** mail cash, registration, license or record of conviction stubs. Use check or money order.

Information contained on this side of ticket refers to **Traffic Infractions Only.**

▶ **WORKSHOP PRACTICE:** Reading Traffic Signs

To be a safe driver, understand and obey traffic signs. Look at the signs on this page. Write the meaning of each sign. Look back at page 60 if you need help.

1. _____   2. _____   3. _____

4. _____   5. _____   6. _____

7. _____   8. _____   9. _____

▶ **COMPREHENSION:** Circle the Answer

Draw a circle around the correct answer.

1. Which kind of traffic line should never be crossed when driving?

one solid line   one broken line   solid double line

2. At which speed do more accidents happen?

25 miles per hour   45 miles per hour   65 miles per hour

3. Which one has the right of way on a highway?

a car that is already on the highway

a car entering the highway

a truck entering the highway

4. Where are you never allowed to park?

in a tunnel   on the street   in a shopping center

5. How many states require drivers to wear seat belts and use car seats for small children?

all   some   none

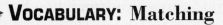

VOCABULARY: Matching

Match the word or phrase in Group B with a definition in Group A.
Write the letter of the correct answer on the line.

Group A	Group B
_____ **1.** This is a person who is walking.	**a.** minimum speed
_____ **2.** This is the front window of a car or truck.	**b.** crosswalk
_____ **3.** This is the slowest speed at which you are allowed to drive.	**c.** pedestrian
_____ **4.** This is where two streets cross each other.	**d.** windshield
_____ **5.** This is an area that is marked with lines for walking across the street.	**e.** intersection

THINKING AND WRITING Imagine what it would be like if there were no traffic laws. People could drive at any speed and go in any direction. In your journal explain why we need traffic laws. Tell which ones you think are most important.

SOCIAL SECURITY

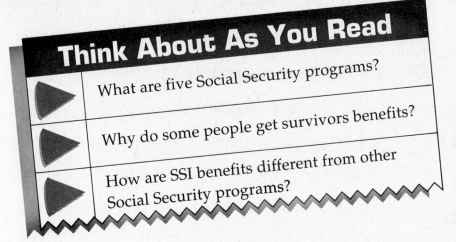

Think About As You Read

▶ What are five Social Security programs?

▶ Why do some people get survivors benefits?

▶ How are SSI benefits different from other Social Security programs?

Survivors benefits are monthly checks that are paid to certain family members of a worker who has died.

Social Security is a federal program that provides monthly income to many people.

Lauren Brown had three children when her husband was killed in an accident. Lauren had a good job, but she depended on her husband's income. She worried about how she would care for her family without his income. Lauren learned that she could get **survivors benefits** from a federal plan called **Social Security**. The Social Security money Lauren receives each month helps her care for her family. In this chapter you will learn how Social Security works and how it may help you.

Social Security helps families like Lauren's.

How Social Security Works

You become part of the Social Security plan when you get a Social Security card. Your card has your Social Security number. Most parents get Social Security cards for their children soon after they are born. If you were born in a different country, you have to fill out a special Social Security form to get a card.

The amount of Social Security money workers can get is based on both the number of years they have worked and their income. You receive Social Security **credits** for each year that you work. You can earn as many as four credits in one year. To receive the most benefits, you have to earn 40 credits. Most people earn these 40 credits by working for ten years. If you have fewer than 40 credits, you will receive fewer benefits.

To receive Social Security benefits, you earn **credits** for the time you spend working.

All Social Security programs are paid for with tax money. Most workers have to pay Social Security taxes, or FICA, to the Internal Revenue Service. Check your paystub to see how much of your income is used to pay the FICA tax.

Workers who earn higher incomes usually receive larger Social Security benefits. Workers who earn less money usually get lower benefits. For most people, Social Security does not provide enough money to pay for all of their needs.

The Social Security agency has a record of your credits and your income. Have your Social Security records checked once in three years. Be sure that your records have the correct information about the number of credits and the amount of money you have earned. If there are mistakes on your records, you may receive lower benefits than you deserve. To check your records, call or visit a Social Security office near your home. A Social Security worker will help you get the information you need. Social Security never charges you for information or services.

Retirement is the period when an older person no longer works.

Medicare is a health insurance program from Social Security. It helps older adults pay for medical care.

A **spouse** is a husband or wife.

Supplemental Security Income (SSI) pays monthly checks to low-income people who are 65 or disabled.

How Social Security Helps People

Social Security has offices in every state. People in every state receive the same Social Security benefits. There are five Social Security programs.

1. Retirement benefits are paid to older people.

2. Medicare is a health insurance program. It is for people 65 or older and for many people with disabilities.

3. Survivors benefits are paid to certain family members if a parent or **spouse** dies.

4. Disability benefits are paid to workers who are disabled and sometimes to their family members.

5. Supplemental Security Income, or **SSI**, benefits are paid to some people with low incomes.

Social Security Programs

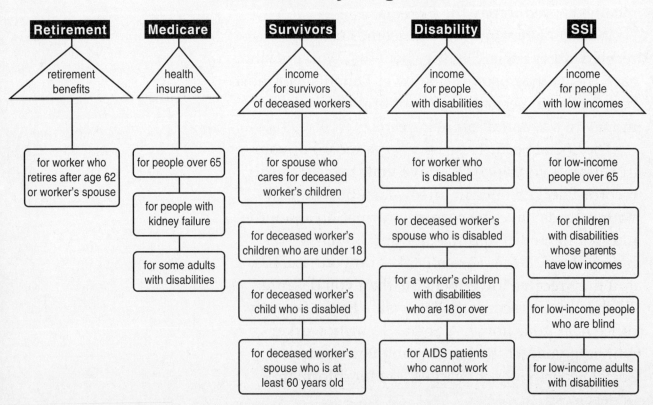

Retirement and Medicare

Most people look forward to getting Social Security retirement benefits. You can receive benefits if you have worked and earned 40 credits. You also have to be old enough to receive retirement benefits. If you were born after 1960, you can receive full benefits after you are 67 years old. If you were born before 1960, call Social Security to learn when you can receive full retirement benefits. You can start to collect benefits at age 62, but you will get less money each month for the rest of your life. A husband or wife who has never worked can collect benefits if the spouse has earned enough work credits.

Most people can get Medicare benefits if they are 65 years old. People of any age who have **kidney failure** can get Medicare. You can also get Medicare benefits if you have received Social Security disability benefits for 24 months. Medicare helps pay hospital bills. People can buy more Medicare insurance to help pay their doctor bills.

When a person's kidneys stop working, this sickness is called **kidney failure**. Kidneys help remove wastes from the blood.

Social Security helps people enjoy their retirement.

Survivors Benefits

Survivors benefits are paid to certain family members of a **deceased** worker. The deceased worker had to pay Social Security taxes and earn at least six credits in order for the family to get survivors benefits. There are four groups of people who can get survivors benefits.

1. The spouse who takes care of the deceased worker's children can get benefits. Those children have to be disabled or under age 16.

2. The deceased worker's children can get benefits. The children have to be under 18. They can be under 19 if they are full-time students. They cannot be married.

3. A deceased worker's child who is disabled will get benefits until that child marries. The child's disability must have started before age 22.

4. A spouse can get survivors benefits starting at age 60.

A **deceased** person has died.

Social Security programs help people with disabilities.

Disability and SSI Benefits

Disability benefits are paid to people with **severe** disabilities. The Social Security agency decides whether the disability is severe. People with disabilities who work at good jobs and earn good salaries cannot get disability benefits. There are four groups of people who may get disability benefits.

1. Workers who become disabled after they have earned enough credits may get benefits.

2. A deceased worker's spouse who is disabled may get benefits.

3. Children with disabilities who are over age 18 may get benefits if one of their parents has enough credits.

4. People who cannot work because they have AIDS or **HIV infection** may get benefits.

You can apply for benefits as soon as you become disabled. If you can receive disability benefits, your payments will begin after six months. You can get benefits until you are able to return to work. Some people receive benefits for many years.

SSI benefits are paid to help people with low incomes. People who are blind, disabled, or over age 65 can get SSI benefits. Low-income parents with children who are disabled can also get benefits. SSI is different from other Social Security programs. You do not have to work and earn credits to get benefits. Instead, you have to show that you have a low income.

Millions of Americans receive money from Social Security each month. During your working years, you pay taxes to this plan. One day you will be able to enjoy the benefits of Social Security.

Severe means very bad or serious. A severe disability is a disability that prevents a person from earning a good salary.

A person with **HIV infection** has the virus that causes AIDS.

Replacing a Lost Social Security Card

The form on page 75 is a sample of the form used to apply for a Social Security card. You can get a real form from the Social Security office. You use the same form if you lose your card and need another one. You also complete the same form if you have changed your name. A change in name can be from a marriage, divorce, or court order.

To replace a Social Security card, you have to show at least one piece of identification that proves who you are. Some forms of identification are a driver's license, school record, hospital record, or a passport. The identification papers will be returned to you. Take or mail your completed form with identification to your nearest Social Security office.

Lauren Brown lost her Social Security card. She completed the application to replace her card. She used her health insurance card for identification. She knew her Social Security number. You keep the same number for life. It is a good idea to memorize your number. Even though you know your Social Security number, you may need to show your card when you get a new job. Study the form on page 75. Notice that on the form, you do not have to complete section 5.

▼ ▼ ▼

Answer the following questions about Lauren's application.

1. Is it acceptable to use a pencil to fill out this form? _____

2. What was Lauren's name at birth? _____

3. Is it acceptable to abbreviate on this form? _____

4. What is Lauren's mother's maiden name? _____

5. What is Lauren's father's name? _____

6. What was the name Lauren used on her last Social Security card?

_____

SOCIAL SECURITY ADMINISTRATION
Application for a Social Security Card

INSTRUCTIONS

- Print or type using black or blue ink. DO NOT USE PENCIL.
- After you complete this form, take or mail it along with the required documents to your nearest Social Security office.
- If you are completing this form for someone else, answer the questions as they apply to that person. Then, sign your name in question 16.

1 NAME
To Be Shown On Card

▶ Lauren _(FIRST)_   Jessica _(FULL MIDDLE NAME)_   Brown _(LAST)_

FULL NAME AT BIRTH IF OTHER THAN ABOVE

Lauren _(FIRST)_   Jessica _(FULL MIDDLE NAME)_   Johnson _(LAST)_

OTHER NAMES USED

2 MAILING ADDRESS
Do Not Abbreviate

▶ 135 Pearl Street   Apartment 2H
STREET ADDRESS, APT. NO., PO BOX, RURAL ROUTE NO.

Jersey City _(CITY)_   New Jersey _(STATE)_   07304 _(ZIP CODE)_

3 CITIZENSHIP
(Check One)

- [x] U.S. Citizen
- [ ] Legal Alien Allowed To Work
- [ ] Legal Alien Not Allowed To Work
- [ ] Foreign Student Allowed Restricted Employment
- [ ] Conditionally Legalized Alien Allowed To Work
- [ ] Other (See Instructions On Page 2)

4 SEX

- [ ] Male
- [x] Female

5 RACE/ETHNIC DESCRIPTION
(Check One Only – Voluntary)

- [ ] Asian, Asian-American Or Pacific Islander
- [ ] Hispanic
- [x] Black (Not Hispanic)
- [ ] North American Indian Or Alaskan Native
- [ ] White (Not Hispanic)

6 DATE OF BIRTH   8/24/63 _(MONTH DAY YEAR)_

7 PLACE OF BIRTH (Do Not Abbreviate)   Trenton _(CITY)_   New Jersey _(STATE OR FOREIGN COUNTRY)_

8 MOTHER'S MAIDEN NAME   Donna _(FIRST)_   Mary _(FULL MIDDLE NAME)_   Mason _(LAST NAME AT HER BIRTH)_

9 FATHER'S NAME   Henry _(FIRST)_   Paul _(FULL MIDDLE NAME)_   Johnson _(LAST)_

10 Has the person in item 1 ever received a Social Security number before?
- [x] Yes (If "yes," answer questions 11-13.)
- [ ] No (If "no," go on to question 14.)
- [ ] Don't Know (If "don't know," go on to question 14.)

11 Enter the Social Security number previously assigned to the person listed in item 1.

888 – 99 – 7777

12 Enter the name shown on the most recent Social Security card issued for the person listed in item 1.

Lauren _(FIRST)_   Jessica _(MIDDLE)_   Brown _(LAST)_

13 Enter any different date of birth if used on an earlier application for a card. _____ _(MONTH DAY YEAR)_

14 TODAY'S DATE ▶ 3/1/94 _(MONTH DAY YEAR)_   **15 DAYTIME PHONE NUMBER** ▶ (609) 555-1212 _(AREA CODE)_

Deliberately furnishing (or causing to be furnished) false information on this application is a crime punishable by fine or imprisonment, or both.

16 YOUR SIGNATURE

▶ _Lauren Jessica Brown_

17 YOUR RELATIONSHIP TO THE PERSON IN ITEM 1 IS:
- [x] Self
- [ ] Natural or Adoptive Parent
- [ ] Legal Guardian
- [ ] Other (Specify) _____

WORKSHOP PRACTICE: Applying for a Social Security Card

Complete a sample application for a Social Security card for yourself or a family member. You can look back at Lauren's completed form in the Life Skills Workshop on page 75.

SOCIAL SECURITY ADMINISTRATION
Application for a Social Security Card

1 NAME
To Be Shown On Card

FIRST   FULL MIDDLE NAME   LAST

FULL NAME AT BIRTH IF OTHER THAN ABOVE

FIRST   FULL MIDDLE NAME   LAST

OTHER NAMES USED

2 MAILING ADDRESS
Do Not Abbreviate

STREET ADDRESS, APT. NO., PO BOX, RURAL ROUTE NO.

CITY   STATE   ZIP CODE

3 CITIZENSHIP
(Check One)

☐ U.S. Citizen   ☐ Legal Alien Allowed To Work   ☐ Legal Alien Not Allowed To Work   ☐ Foreign Student Allowed Restricted Employment   ☐ Conditionally Legalized Alien Allowed To Work   ☐ Other (See Instructions On Page 2)

4 SEX

☐ Male   ☐ Female

5 RACE/ETHNIC DESCRIPTION
(Check One Only – Voluntary)

☐ Asian, Asian-American Or Pacific Islander   ☐ Hispanic   ☐ Black (Not Hispanic)   ☐ North American Indian Or Alaskan Native   ☐ White (Not Hispanic)

6 DATE OF BIRTH

MONTH DAY YEAR

7 PLACE OF BIRTH
(Do Not Abbreviate)

CITY   STATE OR FOREIGN COUNTRY

8 MOTHER'S MAIDEN NAME

FIRST   FULL MIDDLE NAME   LAST NAME AT HER BIRTH

9 FATHER'S NAME

FIRST   FULL MIDDLE NAME   LAST

10 Has the person in item 1 ever received a Social Security number before?

☐ Yes (If "yes," answer questions 11-13.)   ☐ No (If "no," go on to question 14.)   ☐ Don't Know (If "don't know," go on to question 14.)

11 Enter the Social Security number previously assigned to the person listed in item 1.

☐☐☐ – ☐☐ – ☐☐☐☐

12 Enter the name shown on the most recent Social Security card issued for the person listed in item 1.

FIRST   MIDDLE   LAST

13 Enter any different date of birth if used on an earlier application for a card.

MONTH   DAY   YEAR

14 TODAY'S DATE ▶ _____
MONTH   DAY   YEAR

15 DAYTIME PHONE NUMBER ▶ ( )
AREA CODE

Deliberately furnishing (or causing to be furnished) false information on this application is a crime punishable by fine or imprisonment, or both.

16 YOUR SIGNATURE

▶ _____

17 YOUR RELATIONSHIP TO THE PERSON IN ITEM 1 IS:

☐ Self   ☐ Natural or Adoptive Parent   ☐ Legal Guardian   ☐ Other (Specify)

_____

VOCABULARY: Writing with Vocabulary Words

Use five or more of the following words or phrases to write a paragraph that tells about the Social Security system.

Social Security
retirement
survivors benefits
Medicare
disability
deceased
credits

_____

_____

_____

_____

_____

_____

_____

 **COMPREHENSION:** Write the Answer

Write one or more sentences to answer each question.

1. Where does the government get money to pay Social Security benefits?

_____

2. How many credits does a person need to have in order to receive the most Social Security benefits? _____

_____

3. Who can get Social Security disability benefits? _____

_____

4. Who can get Social Security survivors benefits? _____

_____

5. Who can get Supplemental Security Income? _____

_____

THINKING AND WRITING Do you think it is fair that workers who earn higher incomes will receive more Social Security benefits than workers who earn less money? In your journal explain why you think this system is fair or unfair.

EIGHT

VOTING IN ELECTIONS

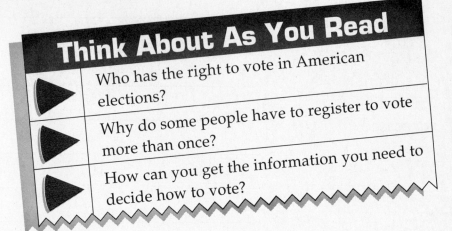

Think About As You Read

▶ Who has the right to vote in American elections?

▶ Why do some people have to register to vote more than once?

▶ How can you get the information you need to decide how to vote?

Van Deng Cong moved to the United States from Vietnam. In Vietnam he did not enjoy freedom of speech. It was dangerous to speak against the government. He could be sent to jail without a fair trial. Van Deng left his country and moved to the United States. After Van Deng became a citizen, he was proud to vote in American **elections**.

Americans choose their leaders by voting in elections. Each time you vote, you have a voice in your government.

An **election** is an event in which people choose leaders by voting.

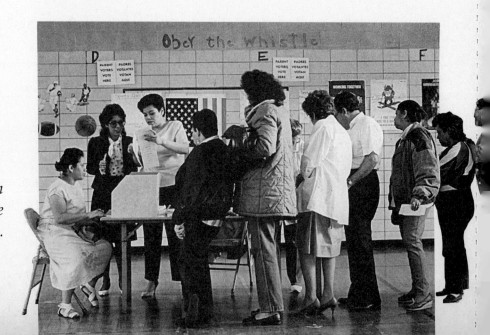

Americans vote in elections to choose government leaders.

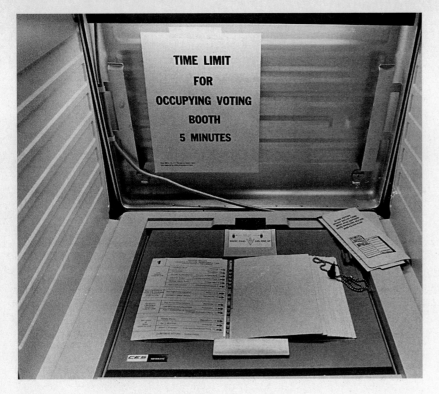

TIME LIMIT
FOR
OCCUPYING VOTING
BOOTH
5 MINUTES

Different voting areas may use different types of voting machines.

Your Right to Vote

The Constitution gives Americans the right to vote. There are four rules about who can vote.

1. You have to be 18 or older.

2. You have to be an American citizen. If you were not born in the United States, you can become a citizen through Immigration and Naturalization Services, or INS.

3. You have to live in your state for a certain amount of time. Each state has its own laws about the amount of time you have to live there before you can vote.

4. You have to register to vote.

The Constitution protects your right to vote. You cannot lose your right to vote because of your race, sex, or religion. You cannot lose it because you speak against the government. But people who are in prison lose their right to vote.

You need to register before you can vote in an election.

Your right to vote allows you to vote in federal, state, and local elections. You can vote to help choose the President of the United States. You can also vote for many other leaders and lawmakers.

In an election every vote counts. The **candidate** who gets the most votes becomes the winner. Sometimes a candidate wins by only a few votes. Your vote can help a candidate win or lose.

A **candidate** is a person who is trying to get elected to a job in government.

Register to Vote

In 49 states people have to register in order to vote. North Dakota is the only state where you do not have to register before you can vote.

Every state has its own rules about how to register. Most states allow you to register in person or by mail. Some states allow you to register at banks, public schools, and libraries. You have to complete a voter registration form. You do not pay a fee when you register. The Life Skills Workshop in this chapter shows you how to complete a voter registration form.

Find out the rules for voter registration in your state. Learn how many days before an election you have to register to vote. In some states you can get information by calling a voter registration office. In other states you can get information by calling the Board of Elections. You can also get information by calling the nearest office of the League of Women Voters.

In some states when you register to vote, you can also join a **political party**. There may be a place on your registration form to register to be a member of a political party. You do not have to pay to join a political party. The **Democratic** and **Republican** parties are the two largest political parties in our nation. Members of political parties work together to reach goals. They work together to help their candidates win elections. You may want to do **volunteer work** to help your political party. You do not have to join a political party when you register to vote.

Sometimes you have to register to vote more than once. If you do not vote for a few years, you will have to register again. Complete a new voter registration form if you want to change your political party. If you move to a new address or change your name, you need to register again.

A **political party** is a large group of people who have similar beliefs about government. This group will try to get members of their party elected.

The **Democratic Party** is one of the two largest American political parties.

The **Republican Party** is the other large political party.

Volunteer work is work that people are not paid to do. The work is done to help an organization.

Candidates try hard to build support.

Becoming a Smart Voter

To be a smart voter, you need information about the different candidates in an election. Learn what each candidate hopes to do after winning the election. Learn about the work the candidates have done before the election **campaign**. Use this information to decide how to vote.

You can get information about candidates by listening to news reports. Listen to the speeches the candidates make on TV and radio to learn their ideas. Newspaper and magazine articles can help you learn about the candidates.

As you find information, learn the difference between facts and **opinions** about the candidates. Facts are true information. Opinions are statements that tell you what some people think about the candidate. For example, an opinion might be that one candidate is smarter than the other. You can disagree with the opinions other people may have about a candidate. Use the facts about the candidates to form your own opinions. In your opinion one candidate may be a better choice than the other. Your opinions will help you decide how to vote.

A smart voter also pays attention to campaign ads. There are ads on radio and TV and in newspapers. Sometimes ads contain information that is not completely true. By learning the facts about a candidate, you will know when the ads are correct.

In most states only members of a political party can vote in **primary elections**. In the primary election, you vote for a person to be the candidate of your political party. Your party's winning candidate will run against the candidate from the other party in the main election. In most states to vote in a primary, you have to be registered as a Democrat or as a Republican. Learn as much as you can about each candidate before voting in a primary election.

A **campaign** is all the ways a candidate seeks support to win an election.

An **opinion** is a belief that tells how you think or feel about a person or event. The sentence "George Washington was our best president" is an opinion.

In a **primary election**, members of a political party elect their candidates for the main election.

Before an election, you may receive voting information in the mail. This information will tell you when and where to vote. You can also get this information by calling the Board of Elections. The League of Women Voters also provides this information. Your place to vote is called a **polling place**. You can find copies of the **ballot** in local newspapers. Study the ballot. Decide how you want to vote before going to your polling place on Election Day.

At every polling place, Americans vote with secret ballots. No one will know who you vote for. You have the right to vote for the candidate that you think is best.

Smart voters do not vote for candidates because of their race, sex, religion, or good looks. They do not vote for a candidate because their friends tell them to. They choose the candidates that they think will do the best job.

Every American has one vote on Election Day. When you vote, you have the same power as every other citizen in the nation. Use your vote to choose good leaders for America.

A **polling place** is the place where you vote. You are allowed to vote at only one polling place.

A **ballot** is a form used for voting. This form lists all the candidates.

How to Vote in an Election

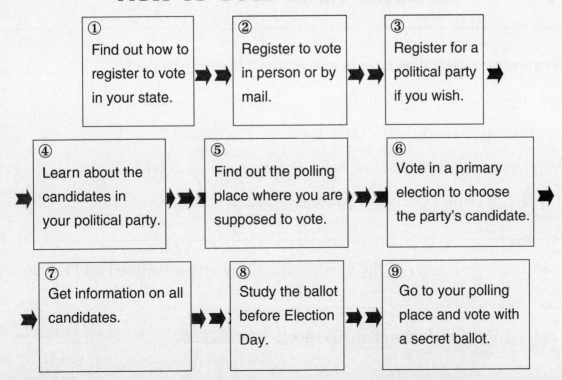

① Find out how to register to vote in your state.

② Register to vote in person or by mail.

③ Register for a political party if you wish.

④ Learn about the candidates in your political party.

⑤ Find out the polling place where you are supposed to vote.

⑥ Vote in a primary election to choose the party's candidate.

⑦ Get information on all candidates.

⑧ Study the ballot before Election Day.

⑨ Go to your polling place and vote with a secret ballot.

Completing a Voter Registration Form

In every state except North Dakota, you have to register in order to vote. To register, you complete a **voter registration form**. You do not need to pay to register. It is against the law to charge a fee for registration. In most states you need to register at least 30 days before an election. After you complete the form, you can take it to the registration office. Most states allow you to mail the form to the registration office.

The voter registration form on page 85 is a sample of the form used by citizens in California. Most states ask for similar information on their registration forms. Read the form and the instructions for completing the **affidavit**. An affidavit is a legal form. **Perjury** is to swear to something that is not true. Perjury is against the law. Write only true information on a voter registration form. Note that you do not have to write your phone number on this voter registration form. It is marked "optional." If you do not want to join a political party, you can mark "Decline to State." This means you do not want to mark a certain political party.

After Van Deng Cong became an American citizen, he registered to vote. Then he moved to a new address. So he had to register again.

▼ ▼ ▼

Use Van Deng's voter registration form to answer the following questions.

1. In what county does Van Deng live? _____

2. Which political party did Van Deng join? _____

3. Has Van Deng registered to vote before? yes _____ no _____

4. What was Van Deng's previous address? _____

_____

5. Was Van Deng a member of the Democratic Party when he lived on Prairie

Avenue? yes _____ no _____

6. Who helped Van Deng complete his form? _____

For U.S. Citizens Only

STATE OF CALIFORNIA
AFFIDAVIT OF REGISTRATION

1 NAME (First) (Middle) (Last)
Optional ☒ Mr. ☐ Mrs. ☐ Miss ☐ Ms.
Van Deng Cong

2 RESIDENCE (Number – Street – Apartment No.)
260 West 6th Street Apt. 3K
City — County — ZIP Code
Los Angeles Los Angeles County 90057

3 If no street address, describe location of residence: (cross streets, route, box, section, township, range, etc.)

4 MAILING ADDRESS (if different from residence)
City — State — ZIP Code

5 DATE OF BIRTH (Month – Day – Year)
09-06-59

6 BIRTHPLACE (U.S. State or Foreign Country)
Vietnam

7 POLITICAL PARTY (check one)
☐ American Independent Party
☒ Democratic Party
☐ Green Party
☐ Libertarian Party
☐ Peace and Freedom Party
☐ Republican Party
☐ Decline to State
☐ Other (Specify)

8 OCCUPATION
salesperson

9 Telephone (Optional)
Area Code *(213) 555-6240*

10 Not applicable in this County

11 HAVE YOU EVER BEEN REGISTERED TO VOTE? Yes ☒ No ☐
If yes, complete this section to the best of your knowledge concerning your **most recent** registration.

Name (as registered)
Van Deng Cong
Former Address
403 Prairie Avenue
City — County — State
Los Angeles Los Angeles County CA
Political Party
Democratic

READ THIS STATEMENT AND WARNING PRIOR TO SIGNING
I am a citizen of the United States and will be at least 18 years of age at the time of the next election. I am not imprisoned or on parole for the conviction of a felony. I certify under **penalty of perjury** under the laws of the State of California that the information on this affidavit is true and correct.

WARNING
Perjury is punishable by imprisonment in state prison for two, three or four years. §126 Penal Code

12 SIGNATURE — Sign on line in box below.

▶ *Van Deng cong*

▶ Date *10-05-94*   *59 AD 609000*

13 If someone helps fill out or keeps this form, see #13 instructions below.
(213) 555-3282
Tim Collins   *10-05-94*

INSTRUCTIONS FOR COMPLETING THE AFFIDAVIT

TYPE OR PRINT IN INK: Read instructions and information carefully. Only your "signature" should be written; all other information should be printed or typed.

WARNING—STATEMENT UNDER PENALTY OF PERJURY: Be sure you read the statement and warning above the signature line **prior** to signing your complete name. You must also date the affidavit. If you are 17 years of age, you may register to vote provided you will be 18 on or before the date of the next election.

1 Print your full name—first, middle, last.

2 Print your complete RESIDENCE ADDRESS (not P.O. box) including city and zip code. Enter street name to include North, South, East, West, if appropriate, and indicate whether it is a street, avenue, road, lane, drive, way, circle, etc.

3 If no street address, describe location of residence: (cross streets, route, box, section, township, range, etc.)

4 Print your complete mailing address if it is different from your residence address. Be sure to enter the route or box number, if any, and zip code.

5 Print your complete date of birth (month/day/year).

6 Print the name of the state in U.S.A. or foreign country where you were born.

7 IMPORTANT—POLITICAL PARTY: Place an "X" in the box preceding the qualified political party with which you wish to affiliate. You may print the name of an unqualified political party with which you wish to affiliate after "Other," or you may register as "Decline to State." IF YOU DO NOT AFFILIATE WITH A QUALIFIED POLITICAL PARTY, YOU WILL RECEIVE A NONPARTISAN BALLOT AND WILL NOT BE ALLOWED TO VOTE FOR PARTY CANDIDATES AT THE PRIMARY ELECTION.

8 Print your specific occupation (such as nurse, carpenter, homemaker, etc.).

9 OPTIONAL: Telephone number is optional. This number becomes public record if given. Please include Area Code.

10 Not applicable in this county (for official use only).

11 PRIOR REGISTRATION: If you have ever been registered to vote, complete this portion to the best of your knowledge concerning your most recent registration.

12 Sign your name as printed in Box 1. Date the affidavit below the signature box in the space provided.

13 Any person who helps someone fill out this form must include in Box 13 his/her signature and date.

▶ **WORKSHOP PRACTICE: Complete a Voter Registration Form**

Complete the sample voter registration form on this page.
Remember that this form is a sample. You cannot use it for
your registration in any state. You have to use your state's
voter registration form to register to vote.

PRINT IN INK   For U.S. Citizens Only

STATE OF CALIFORNIA

AFFIDAVIT OF REGISTRATION

1 Optional ☐Mr. ☐Mrs. ☐Miss ☐Ms.
   NAME (First   Middle   Last)

2 RESIDENCE (Number – Street – Apartment No.)

   City   County   ZIP Code

3 If no street address, describe location of residence: (cross streets, route, box, section, township, range, etc.)

4 MAILING ADDRESS (if different from residence)

   City   State   ZIP Code

5 DATE OF BIRTH (Month – Day – Year)   **8** OCCUPATION

6 BIRTHPLACE (U.S. State or Foreign Country)

7 POLITICAL PARTY (check one)   **9** Telephone (Optional)
   ☐ American Independent Party   Area Code
   ☐ Democratic Party   (   )
   ☐ Green Party   **10** Not applicable in this
   ☐ Libertarian Party   County
   ☐ Peace and Freedom Party
   ☐ Republican Party
   ☐ Decline to State
   ☐ Other (Specify) _____

11 HAVE YOU EVER BEEN REGISTERED TO VOTE? Yes☐ No☐
   If yes, complete this section to the best of your knowledge concerning your **most recent** registration.

   Name (as registered)

   Former Address

   City   County   State

   Political Party

   READ THIS STATEMENT AND WARNING PRIOR TO SIGNING
   I am a citizen of the United States and will be at least 18 years of age at the time of the next election. I am not imprisoned or on parole for the conviction of a felony. I certify under **penalty of perjury** under the laws of the State of California that the information on this affidavit is true and correct.
   WARNING
   Perjury is punishable by imprisonment in state prison for two, three or four years. §126 Penal Code

12 SIGNATURE — Sign on line in box below.

   Date   59 AD 609000

13 If someone helps fill out or keeps this form, see #13 instructions below.   (   )

SAMPLE

▶ **VOCABULARY: Find the Meaning**

On the line write the word or phrase that best completes each sentence.

1. People vote in _____ to choose leaders.

       campaigns   elections   opinions

2. The people who are trying to get elected are the _____.

       employers   citizens   candidates

3. A _____ is the place where you go to vote.

ballot   polling place   court

4. The form that lists the candidates is called a _____ .

poll   opinion   ballot

5. All the ways a candidate seeks support to win an election are called the

_____ .

campaign   political party   volunteer work

 COMPREHENSION: Finish the Paragraph
Use the following words or phrases to finish the paragraph.
Write the words you choose on the correct lines.

citizen
speeches
news reports
government
Constitution
register
political party
race
opinions

To vote in elections, you have to be an American

_____ . The _____

protects your right to vote. You cannot lose your right to

vote because of your sex, _____ , or

religion. Before you can vote, you have to

_____ . When you register, you can

become a member of a _____ . You

can get information about the candidates from

_____ and _____ .

Learn the difference between facts and

_____ about the candidates. By

using your right to vote, you have a voice in the

_____ .

 **THINKING AND WRITING**   Each year on Election Day, many people do not vote. Do you think it is important for every citizen to register and vote? In your journal explain why or why not.

87

Glossary

affidavit A legal form. page 84

affirmative action programs Programs that give a certain number of jobs to women, members of minority groups, and people with disabilities. page 39

agencies Large groups of people in the government that work together to do certain kinds of work. page 8

Aid to Families with Dependent Children (AFDC) A program that provides money to low-income families with children. page 17

amendments Laws that have been added to the Constitution. page 27

application A written form used to get permission to do something. page 47

ballot A form used for voting. page 83

Bill of Rights The first ten amendments that were added to the Constitution. page 27

birth certificate A paper from a local government that has information about a person's name, birth, and parents. page 17

branches Parts of a whole. There are three branches of government. page 6

campaign All the ways a candidate seeks support to win an election. page 82

candidate A person who is trying to get elected to a job in government. page 80

citizens People who are members of a nation and have the rights of that nation. page 19

civil courts Courts that decide how to solve problems between people. page 29

commit To do a crime. page 29

Congress The part of the government that makes the laws for the United States. page 7

constitution A plan for government. page 6

credits Social Security points you earn for the time you spend working. page 69

criminal courts Courts that decide if an accused person broke a law and committed a crime like murder or robbery. page 29

crosswalk An area in an intersection that is marked with lines. People walk across the street at this marked area. page 62

deceased Dead. page 72

defendant The person who is being sued or accused of a crime. page 31

Democratic Party One of the two largest American political parties. page 81

Department of Housing and Urban Development (HUD) A federal government agency that helps people with low incomes find housing that they can afford. page 21

department of social services A state agency that helps people get many kinds of services. page 21

disability A problem that makes a person less able to do certain things. page 37

discriminate against To treat a person unfairly. page 37

discrimination Treating people unfairly because of age, sex, race, religion, or disability. page 36

double park To park to the left of cars that are already in the parking lane. It is against the law to double park. page 62

driving under the influence (DUI) To drink alcohol or use drugs and drive. page 52

driving while intoxicated (DWI) To drink alcohol and drive. page 51

election An event in which people choose leaders by voting. page 78

employer The person or business that hires you for a job. page 36

Equal Employment Opportunity Commission (EEOC) A federal agency that makes sure that laws against job discrimination are obeyed. page 41

evidence Something that helps prove a person did a crime. page 29

executive branch One of the three branches of government. The executive branch carries out the laws written by the legislative branch. page 7

expire To come to the end of the period of time when something can be used. page 49

federal government The government for the entire nation. page 6

fee The money paid for a service. page 47

fire hydrant A pump used to provide water to fight fires. page 57

Food and Drug Administration (FDA) A federal agency that checks the safety of foods, medicines, and make-up. page 20

guilty To be proved that a person did a crime. page 27

HIV infection The virus that causes AIDS. page 73

illegal Against the law. page 37

illegal aliens People who come to the United States from other nations without the permission of the United States government. page 40

Immigration and Naturalization Services (INS) A federal agency that helps people from other nations get legal papers to live in the United States. It also helps people become American citizens. page 19

intersection A place where two streets cross each other. page 58

jury A group of people who decide if an accused person is guilty of a crime. page 30

kidney failure A sickness in which a person's kidneys stop working. page 71

learner's permit A paper that gives you permission to practice driving before you get your driver's license. page 47

legislative Lawmaking. One of the three branches of government. page 7

legislators Lawmakers. page 5

local governments The governments for cities, towns, counties, villages, and other regions in a state. page 6

maiden name A woman's last name when she was born. page 22

Medicaid A program to help people with low incomes pay for medical care. page 17

Medicare A health insurance program from Social Security. It helps older adults pay for medical care. page 70

minimum speed The slowest speed at which you are allowed to drive. page 61

minority groups Groups of people in a nation that are not like most people in that nation. For example, the difference may be race or religion. page 38

Miranda warning The warning that police must tell all people they arrest. It tells accused people of their rights. page 30

motor vehicle department The state agency that carries out traffic laws and helps people get driver's licenses. page 47

national origin The country where you were born. page 38

notary A person who can stamp a form to prove that you signed it. page 31

opinion A belief that tells how you think or feel about a person or event. page 82

pedestrian A person who walks. page 63

perjury Swearing to something that is not true. Perjury is against the law. page 84

plaintiff The person who is bringing a case to court. page 32

political party A large group of people who have similar beliefs about government. This group tries to get members of their party elected. page 81

polling place The place where you vote. page 83

prejudiced Having bad ideas about others before knowing them. page 30

primary election An election in which members of a political party elect their candidates for the main election. page 82

registration A card, paper, or sticker from the state motor vehicle department that shows who owns a car. page 48

renew To sign up for a license or car registration again so it can continue to be used for a certain period of time. page 48

representatives Lawmakers who are elected to serve in the House of Representatives. page 7

Republican Party One of the two largest American political parties. page 81

retaliation Getting even. page 42

retirement The period when an older person no longer works. page 70

revoked Taken away and can never be used again. page 49

right of way The right to enter the highway or road before other vehicles. page 63

safety inspection To check a car for safety. page 49

senators Lawmakers who are elected to serve in the Senate. page 7

severe Very bad or serious. page 73

sexual harassment Acts and words about sex that make you feel uncomfortable. page 38

small claims courts Civil courts used to solve problems that do not involve very large amounts of money. page 31

Social Security A federal program that provides monthly income to many people. page 68

solid Without any breaks, such as a solid line. page 58

spouse A husband or wife. page 70

state employment agency A state agency that can help a person find a job. page 18

sue To take someone to court. page 40

Supplemental Security Income (SSI) A Social Security program that pays monthly checks to low-income people who are 65 or disabled. page 70

survivors benefits Monthly checks that are paid to certain family members of a worker who has died. page 68

suspended Cannot be used for a certain period of time. page 49

tinted Coated to be made darker, such as tinted windows. page 59

trial An event where a person accused of a crime is judged in a court. page 26

turn signals The flashing lights on a car that are used to show other drivers when you are making a left or right turn. page 49

unemployment insurance If you lose your job, this state program may pay part of your salary while you look for work. page 18

violation Breaking a driving law. page 49

vital records office A government office that keeps birth and death certificates. page 22

volunteer work Work that people are not paid to do. page 81

windshield The front window of a car or a truck. page 57

witnesses People who have seen an accident. page 53

workers' compensation A state program that may pay part of your salary and medical bills if you get hurt or sick while working. page 18

yield To allow another person or vehicle to enter the road or highway before you. page 63

Chapter 1

Pages 12–13 Workshop

1. Lawton Chiles

2. a cigarette tax

3. More people will try to stop smoking if cigarettes are more expensive, and the tax will give the state more money to spend.

4. United States Representative
United States House of Representatives
Washington, DC 20515

Page 14 Workshop Practice

Letters will vary. Write your letter neatly, spell correctly, and be sure to sign your name. Put your address at the top of the page.

Page 15 Comprehension

1. federal

2. state

3. state, local

4. legislative

5. income

Page 15 Vocabulary

1. b

2. c

3. a

4. e

5. d

Chapter 2

Pages 22–23 Workshop

1. to get a passport

2. Pulaski County

3. Butler

4. $5.00

Page 24 Workshop Practice

Answers will vary. Be sure to include all the information in your letter. You can look in the phone book or check in the library to find the address of the vital records office that you need.

Pages 24–25 Comprehension

1. True

2. False; Local governments keep records of births, deaths, marriages, and divorces.

3. True

4. True

5. False; The federal government has an agency to make sure new medicines are safe.

Page 25 Vocabulary

1. Medicaid

2. state employment agency

3. citizens

4. workers' compensation

5. Department of Housing and Urban Development

6. Food and Drug Administration

Chapter 3

Pages 32–33 Workshop

1. Alice Dolan

2. Anatoly Karpov

3. $54.10

4. no

5. a judge

Page 34 Workshop Practice

IN THE DISTRICT COURT OF THE STATE OF OREGON
FOR THE COUNTY OF MARION
SMALL CLAIMS DEPARTMENT

PLEASE PRINT LEGIBLY

Your Name
Your Address
City, State Zip   Plaintiff   No. _____
Address (include zip code)
Phone   CLAIM AND NOTICE OF CLAIM
Telephone
                    vs.
Freshway Cleaners
1800 Main Street
Salem, Oregon 97301   Defendant
Address (include zip code)
555-3313
Telephone

I, Plaintiff, claim that on or about _today's date_ , 19___ , the above named Defendant of _Marion_ County, Oregon, owed me the sum of $ _150_ , and this sum is still owing for _payment for a coat that was ruined by Freshway Cleaners._ .

Pages 34–35 Vocabulary

1. amendments   3. civil
2. criminal   4. jury

Page 35 Comprehension

1. The Bill of Rights was added to the Constitution to make sure that important rights would be protected for every person in the nation.
2. The Bill of Rights promises freedom of religion to all. You may pray when and how you choose.
3. It means that you cannot be treated differently because of your sex, race, age, or disability.
4. The Miranda warning is the warning police must tell all people they arrest. It tells accused people of their rights.

Chapter 4

Pages 42–43 Workshop

1. Smith's Box Company
2. typing
3. 65 words a minute
4. 50 words a minute
5. She feels she was not hired because she is deaf.

Page 44 Workshop Practice

Check "sex" as the cause of discrimination. Answers will vary. Include the idea that Janet feels she was fired because she is a woman and not because she is a slow or a poor worker.

Page 45 Vocabulary

Answers will vary. You may use more than one vocabulary word in a sentence.

Page 45 Comprehension

People may face discrimination because of their age, race, sex, religion, <u>disability</u>, or <u>national</u> <u>origin</u>. People may face <u>job</u> discrimination from employers. An employer cannot refuse to hire a <u>pregnant</u> woman. People may face <u>housing</u> discrimination when they want to buy or rent a home. The first important law to end discrimination was the <u>Civil Rights Act</u> of 1964.

Chapter 5

Pages 53–54 Workshop

1. Do not leave the place where the accident took place.
2. Cover the injured person with a blanket or coat and call an ambulance and a rescue team.
3. Name, address, and phone number of each driver and each passenger; the vehicle registration number, license plate number, make, model, year, and color for each car; each driver's insurance policy number and name of insurance company.
4. ones that cause damage to cars and property, or that injure or kill people
5. Leave your name, address, phone number, and license number on that car's windshield. Report the accident to the police and your insurance company.

Page 55 Workshop Practice

Answers will vary. Include the following things Jim has to do: turn on the emergency flashing lights, call an ambulance and the police, and take care of the injured people.

Jim and the other driver should be ready to explain to the police what happened and exchange information about themselves and their insurance.

Pages 55–56 Comprehension

1. True
2. False; After you move to a new state, you will need to find out how to get a driver's license in the new state.
3. True
4. False; Drivers are not allowed to pass a stopped school bus when children are getting on and off.
5. True

Page 56 Vocabulary

1. suspended
2. revoked
3. driving while intoxicated
4. registration
5. expired

Chapter 6

Pages 64–65 Workshop

1. 1988 Ford
2. March 14
3. Clerk of the Court
4. by March 14
5. $25.00

Page 66 Workshop Practice

1. No U-Turn
2. No Right Turn
3. No Left Turn
4. Merging Traffic Entering from Right
5. School Crossing
6. Right Lane Ends
7. Slippery When Wet
8. Hill Ahead
9. Pedestrian Crossing

Pages 66–67 Comprehension

1. solid double line
2. 65 miles per hour
3. a car that is already on the highway

4. in a tunnel
5. all

Page 67 Vocabulary

1. c
2. d
3. a
4. e
5. b

Chapter 7

Pages 74–75 Workshop

1. no
2. Lauren Jessica Johnson
3. no
4. Donna Mary Mason
5. Henry Paul Johnson
6. Lauren Jessica Brown

Page 76 Workshop Practice

The answers on the form will vary. Print clearly and fill out the form completely. Do not use any abbreviations on the form.

Page 77 Vocabulary

Answers will vary. You may use more than one vocabulary word in a sentence.

Page 77 Comprehension

1. The government gets money to pay Social Security benefits from Social Security taxes that workers pay.
2. A person needs to earn 40 credits in order to receive the most Social Security benefits.
3. Workers who become disabled, a deceased worker's spouse who is disabled, children with disabilities who are over age 18, and people who cannot work because they have AIDS or HIV infection can get Social Security disability benefits.

4. The spouse who takes care of the deceased worker's children, the deceased worker's children, a deceased worker's child who is disabled, and a spouse age 60 and over can get survivors benefits.

5. People with low incomes who are blind, disabled, or over age 65, or who have children with disabilities, can get Supplemental Security Income.

Chapter 8

Pages **84–85** Workshop

1. Los Angeles County **5.** yes
2. Democratic **6.** Tim Collins
3. yes
4. 403 Prairie Avenue, Los Angeles

Page **86** Workshop Practice

The answers on the form will vary. Print clearly and fill out the form completely.

Pages **86–87** Vocabulary

1. elections **4.** ballot
2. candidates **5.** campaign
3. polling place

Page **87** Comprehension

To vote in elections, you have to be an American <u>citizen</u>. The <u>Constitution</u> protects your right to vote. You cannot lose your right to vote because of your sex, <u>race</u>, or religion. Before you can vote, you have to <u>register</u>. When you register, you can become a member of a <u>political party</u>. You can get information about the candidates from <u>speeches</u> and <u>news reports</u>. Learn the difference between facts and <u>opinions</u> about the candidates. By using your right to vote, you have a voice in the <u>government</u>.